HISTORICAL INSIGHTS
INTO KENT

GW00801974

Historical Insights Into Kent

by

JOYCE A. DRAPER

The Memoir Club

© Joyce A. Draper 2000

First published in 2000 by
The Memoir Club
Whitworth Hall
Spennymoor
County Durham

British Library Cataloguing in
Publication Data.
A catalogue record for this book
is available from the
British Library.

ISBN: 1 84104 018 5

Typeset by George Wishart & Associates, Whitley Bay.
Printed by Lintons Printers, Crook, County Durham.

I would like to dedicate this book to Mark McBrien, for his understanding, encouragement and practical help.

Acknowledgements

Acknowledgements to former colleague Arthur J. Cassell (deceased), Head of History Department, Maidstone School for Girls, who suggested that I should write a book, and to his wife for kindly typing much of the original script 30 years ago.

Apart from expressing my thanks for the front book cover designed by Mark McBrien, I would also like to thank him for the time spent travelling Kent and taking many of the appropriate photographs seen in this book.

Contents

List of Illustrations ix

Foreword xi

Chapter 1   The Romans Came This Way 1

Chapter 2   Craftsmen and Builders 3

Chapter 3   Freshwater Snails 6

Chapter 4   A Hollow Flint 9

Chapter 5   Pickey Lane 12

Chapter 6   The Devil Upside Down 15

Chapter 7   Smuggling 21

Chapter 8   'A Great Trade in Planting of Hops' 23

Chapter 9   'Plum Pottage and Nativity Pies' 27

Chapter 10 Damson Broadcloth 30

Chapter 11 'A Very Queer Small Boy' 33

Chapter 12 L. Munn, Kent 1809 36

Chapter 13 More than Five Hundred Years of History 39

Chapter 14 A Perfect Patchwork 43

Chapter 15 The Ruined Tower 47

Chapter 16 'The Splendour of God' 50

Chapter 17 A Candle Beam 52

Chapter 18 'Three Thousand Tons a Year of Business' 56

Chapter 19 *Swift* and *Sure* – a Recollection 59

Chapter 20 The Shipwrights 63

Chapter 21 To Police Kent 66

Chapter 22 The *Invicta*   68

Chapter 23 'Sweete, Newe and Good'   71

Chapter 24 The *Monthly Mirror*, September 1805   74

Chapter 25 The Viking Ship   77

Chapter 26 The Kentings   80

Chapter 27 St. Martin's, Canterbury   82

Chapter 28 The Gunfounders   84

Chapter 29 Shipway   86

Chapter 30 'New Town' or 'Railway Family'   90

Chapter 31 'Chiefe of Ye Quakers'   93

Chapter 32 *Great Harry*   95

Chapter 33 The 'Bat and Ball'   97

Chapter 34 The Gateway to London   99

Chapter 35 The Kentish Yeoman 103

Chapter 36 'Who'd Ha' Thought It?' 106

Chapter 37 1538 110

Chapter 38 'Bartholomew Fair at the Seaside' 114

List of Illustrations

The Roman Road, Benenden 4

Bethersden marble path, Woodchurch 7

Fossil of an Ammonite, Rose Cottage path, Bethersden 8

Kits Coty House, Aylesford 10

The Wall paintings, Brook Church 17

The lead font, Brookland Church 18

The South Doorway, Barfreystone Church 19

The 'Woolpack' Inn 22

Oast houses, Sheerland, Pluckley 25

Dering windows, Pluckley 28

The Cloth Hall, Smarden 31

The Weavers' houses, Canterbury 32

The 'Sun' Inn, Canterbury 35

The Latin School, Wye College 40

Luddesdown Court 44

St Peter's Cottage, Bethersden 46

Cranbrook Mill 54

Fairfield Church 55

Hoverlloyd, Pegwell Bay 60

Folkestone Harbour 73

A Martello Tower, Hythe 75

The Royal Military Canal, Appledore 76

The Viking Ship, Pegwell Bay 78

The West Doorway, New Romney Church 88

Leeds Castle 101

'The Chequers' Inn, High Halden 108

St Thomas (bas-relief) Godmersham Church 111

St Radegund's Abbey, Bradsole 113

Front cover illustrations (left to right from the top left): the ruins of St Radegund's Abbey; medieval tiles in New Romney Church; The Street, Bethersden; Tenterden Town Hall; Folkestone Harbour; a part of the Manor House (now Palace Farm), Charing; Richborough power station from Richborough Fort (Rutupiae), 1976; the ruined tower, Chart Court Church; 'The Chequers', High Halden; S.E. and Chatham Railway chair; timber-frame house, Cranbrook High Street; Dungeness; mooring hook in the wall at New Romney; Fairfield Church; stained glass window, Barfreystone; the font, St Martin's Church, Canterbury.

Foreword

THIS ENTIRE BOOK of articles has laid dormant for 30 years or so and now the author has added a few passages here and there, to round off that time up to the Millennium. Change in our local history may seem tremendous in our lifetime, however the facts noted by the historian can cover decades or centuries in a few well presented passages on a given subject.

Joyce Draper has given an account on 38 varied subjects of Kentish history, with not only an extraordinary observation of historical fact and local detail, but also with a presentation and style that shows a warmth and understanding of the people and the subject matter.

Rare now, are the people with a gentle spirit, who see with clarity the way things were, the way they are now, and the way they should be. Miss Joyce Draper is one of these people.

Mark McBrien

CHAPTER 1

The Romans Came This Way

A LOCAL PAPER REPORTED: 'the remains of a Roman town house . . . including what may be the best example of Roman wall paintings outside Italy . . . have been uncovered during emergency excavations . . . at Dover.' It was here, in the small bay sheltered by the chalk cliffs, that Julius Caesar nearly set foot in Britain. On 25th August 55 B.C. a small Roman fleet, approaching Dubris (Dover) sighted an army of Britons with their war chariots and horses keeping watch from the cliff top; so the invaders sailed northwards along the coast as far as Deal. Here they dragged their galleys on to the shallow beach. Julius Caesar had landed. Records tell us that this young Roman soldier, a fine swordsman and horseman, only recently acclaimed for his victories in Gaul (France), had come to Britain thinking this isolated, untamed island an easy conquest; almost immediately his fleet was battered by a freak storm and after hasty repairs, he was forced to return to Gaul.

A year later Caesar returned, this time with five legions and a great fleet of galleys. Again he landed at Deal, a standard bearer leaping into the sea and wading ashore holding the Imperial Eagle above his head. Imagine these Roman galleys lined up on the shingle beach. They had their forecastle on the prow and were sometimes rowed by 24 oarsmen and sometimes sailed with main and foresails, drawn up and down on ropes like blinds. They were built for transport not for fighting. The Romans were great soldiers so in spite of the skill of the Britons, with their spears and their chariots and horses, Caesar marched his legions inland to Bigbury near Durovernum (Canterbury), where they stormed the stockades to the hill fort. He went on to cross the Medway and then the Thames. By this time Gaul, only recently conquered, began to rebel and Caesar returned there. It was another hundred years before the Romans came again.

In A.D. 43 Aulus Plautius, with another large fleet of galleys and 40,000 men, sailed into the Wantsum Channel, which then divided the Isle of Thanet from the mainland, and found safe anchorage from

1

storms on a small island, Rutupiae (Richborough). Here he built a double ditch and palisade, a part of which can still be seen today. His large army, his infantry and 2,000 cavalry, his archers and slingers advanced westwards. They fought, as Caesar had done, at Bigbury, and after local skirmishes crossed the River Stour. A fierce two-day battle followed in the Medway valley near Durobrivae (Rochester). However, in spite of the skill of the Britons, praised earlier by Caesar in his writings, the Romans forded the Thames at Westminster at low tide, their shields held high above their heads. Kent had been conquered, and for nearly 400 years it formed part of the Roman Empire. Today in towns and villages there is ample evidence of their culture and way of life.

CHAPTER 2

Craftsmen and Builders

HUGE, GREY FOSSILISED SLABS of Bethersden marble were strewn in the stream bed, some upstream and others downstream of the site of the Roman ford. Under the water and embedded in the steep banks were smaller pieces of ironstone, presumably used as the foundations of this paved causeway. Following, with some difficulty, the line of the Roman road which used this crossing, we found more evidence of its materials: some huge slabs of ironstone, others of slag burnt by iron smelting, and numerous flint nodules and pebbles. Standing by Stream Farm, Benenden and the Kent Ditch at Bodiam Mill, we thought of these Roman road builders some 2,000 years ago. They used stone like the marble and the ironstone quarried nearby and slag, the waste from the local furnaces, and flints, perhaps from the seashore, which then almost reached Benenden.

Their roads, about 20 feet wide, were usually built up of layers of stones and raised above the surrounding land. They followed a series of straight lines sited from hill-top to hill-top by lighting fires, and were built to link towns by the quickest possible route. Many, as at Benenden, are now only footpaths, but others, like Stone Street and Watling Street, form the line of the major 'A' class trunk road from Dubris (Dover) via Durovernum (Canterbury) and Durobrivae (Rochester) to Londinium.

The Romans were not only great road builders; they were architects and town dwellers. Canterbury was a Roman city, an area of 120 acres surrounded by a wall and entered by arched gateways. Today the remains of this seven-feet thick wall built of large coursed flints can be seen beneath the medieval wall. Under Butchery Lane, near the Cathedral, uncovered after centuries of rubbish had been excavated, there is still evidence of the Roman town builders. From the reconstructed wall-picture of the typical villa, it is easy to visualize the Roman girls in their stoles and mantles playing knucklebones in the open courtyard. The hypocaust system reminds us of the technical skill

The Roman Road, Benenden.

of the Romans with their 'under-floor central heating' and the mosaic pavement has a pleasant hand-made appearance. There are small cubes of differently coloured materials, black and orange sandstone, white and grey limestone, yellow and red bricks. To make these tiles, the mosaic worker cut sawn sticks of sandstone into cubes by tapping with a hammer and chisel. For the Romans were great craftsmen. Besides the mosaic workers there were the smiths with their iron tools, the carpenters, shoemakers, fullers and dyers and the potters. We know that in Kent there were the Darenth cloth workers, the Upchurch potters, the Plaxtol tile makers, the stone quarrymen at Lympne, and the Wealden iron smelters. But red-glazed Samian pottery, never made in Kent, was dredged out of the sand near Whitstable, so the Romans were also great traders.

They needed ports. On the cliff-top at Dubris (Dover) there are still the remains of the pharos (lighthouse) built to guide their traders safely into shore, and Portus Lemanis (near present-day Hythe at the foot of the old cliff line) was one of their chief ports. It was probably guarded by a watchtower on the hill above, where Lympne Castle now stands, and linked by a road, Stone Street, with Canterbury.

By 250 A.D., however, the Romans began to fear the Saxon invaders; for Kent was a wealthy part of the Empire and an incentive to raiders and plunderers. So they defended their shores by building forts along the coast at Durobrivae, Reculver, Dubris, and Stutfall (Portus Lemanis); and they reinforced Rutupiae, their original landing place in 43 A.D., with two rows of banks and ditches and an immense stone wall, 10 feet thick. Its ruins can still be seen today looking out over the marshes of the old Wantsum Channel.

CHAPTER 3

Freshwater Snails

F RESHWATER SNAILS, saltwater oysters, giant tropical club mosses are all evidence of the geological history of Kent. Long before the Romans invaded our shores and long before prehistoric man ever lived here, Kent was being formed. In East Kent, 2,000 feet below ground level, miners have dug for coal. Three hundred million years ago the area was a freshwater swamp and the weather was extremely hot and wet. Thick, lush forest trees with fern-like leaves, tree club mosses and horsetails grew in these swamps. They died and decayed, became smothered in fine deposits brought by numerous streams and were eventually compressed into seams of coal, in places nine feet thick. The first borehole was put down at Dover in 1890 and since then 29 seams have been found. By 1971 only three pits were working to provide Richborough Power Station with fuel for electricity; even the local coal merchant's yard was a store for Kent's geological history. Today it is uneconomical to exploit.

With a decrease in the rainfall and fewer rivers bringing silt, the swamps gave way to a freshwater lake, the Wealden Lake, the haunt of the freshwater snails. Some of them died, their bodies decayed and their shells were crushed and ground into a rock. Others died but their shells remained whole long enough to be preserved in stone; these are perfect replicas in shape, size and pattern of those prehistoric creatures and are found in great quantities in the local limestone. With fluctuating rainfall rivers flowed, bringing silt into the lake to form beds of clay. In the low Weald around Biddenden, Smarden and Bethersden, numerous ponds are evidence of past quarrying of this limestone, locally called Bethersden marble, out of these claybeds. The stone pavement of Biddenden street and the footpath in Smarden churchyard are patterned by snails, polished by the feet of villagers. The marble fireplaces seen at Knole House, Sevenoaks and Godinton House, Ashford were polished by craftsmen.

The scene changed a 100 million years ago. Kent became a shallow,

Bethersden marble path, Woodchurch.

saltwater bay. Millions of microscopic creatures lived here. Their calcium carbonate shells made the chalk that is so prominent in our Downlands and the white cliffs along the shore. Studied carefully, chalk consists of white grains mixed with fragments of shells and complete shells of minute sea creatures. Frequently fossil moulds and fossil casts can be found of the ammonite, sea urchins, sponges and oysters. Every disused chalk pit is a geologist's hunting ground.

At this time in its geological history, Kent was affected by the earth movements which were building the Alps and it was raised above sea level and became a land mass to be built up and worn down by rivers, the weather, land animals, plants and later by man into the Kent we

Fossil of an Ammonite, Rose Cottage path, Bethersden.

know. Even today these factors are at work. Freshwater snails are scattered at the foot of the massive tower of Biddenden church; they are crumbling out of the limestone wall. These are perfect casts of the prehistoric snails which lived here 100 million years ago.

CHAPTER 4

A Hollow Flint

A HEAP OF FLINT NODULES, waste flint-flakes and flint axeheads found in the Medway valley at Cuxton, are evidence of a pre-historic workshop. Forty thousand years ago, when Kent was still joined to France, Palaeolithic Man was working in flint; hammering, scraping, chopping and cutting to shape the flint nodules into his tools and weapons. These early inhabitants were nomadic hunters and gatherers, probably only finding shelter in extremely inclement weather, for Britain was still within the grip of the last great Ice Age. In 1935, 24 feet deep in the gravel pits of the Thames valley at Swanscombe, a part of a human skull was found which has become famous as that of the 'Swanscombe Man', although doubts as to its authenticity still remain. In 1955 further excavations were carried out when another human skull bone was discovered along with the fossilized bones of his animals of prey: the bear, horse, deer, rhinoceros and elephant. Today the construction of the Channel Tunnel Link is unearthing new finds. In 1999 a skeleton of a pre-Roman horse was found, tagged and re-buried for future generations to explore.

By 5000 B.C. Kent was separated from France by a narrow channel. New settlers came from Europe, and even from North Africa, in their dugout tree-trunk canoes worked with wooden paddles. These Mesolithic people were nomadic hunters and fishermen. We can trace their wanderings by finding their flint axes in Tovil, Hollingbourne, Allington, Ditton, East Malling, Seal and Ightham, and on the High Rocks escarpment at Tunbridge Wells, where good drainage, a water supply and rocks for shelter provided them with occasional settlement. Only the other day a digger driver handed me a flint axehead he had unearthed while excavating a building site.

Kent's population continued to increase, with more and more settlers arriving from the Continent, from France and from Spain, bringing with them new ideas. These Neolithic settlers in 2000 B.C. were not only flint workers; they were potters, cultivators, herdsmen

Kits Coty House, Aylesford.

and traders; they lived in villages and had a religious culture. At Grovehurst (Sittingbourne), above the Swale, there must have been a complete working community. Excavations have revealed bowl-shaped hut depressions, wattle and daub used for walls, bones and horns of cattle, a sandstone grain rubber, flint tools and a reddish-grey pottery; but their greatest monuments to posterity are their megaliths. Scattered over the Downs are hard rock boulders, some large, others small, called sarsen stones, probably the remnants of deposits which once covered the Chalk Downs. It is possible to count 80 in a half-mile stretch along the Pilgrims' Way to the west of Charing. These stones were used by the Neolithic people for their burial chambers; Kits Coty House, on the Downs above Aylesford, is the finest example of a tomb entrance, with its three upright stones 8-12 feet high and its 10-ton capstone. As Samuel Pepys wrote of it in his diary in 1669, 'But certainly it is a thing of great antiquity and I am mightily glad to see it'. But Kits Coty House is only one in a line of monuments east and west of the Medway; the local Ordnance Survey map plots the White Horse Stone and the Countless Stones at Aylesford, the Coldrum Stones at Trottiscliffe and the Chestnuts at Addington.

Right up to the Roman invasion in 43 A.D., more and more people were crossing the Channel from northern France and the Low Countries. There were the Beaker folk who travelled up the Medway and the Stour and along the North Kent coast. At first they brought their bronze tools with them but eventually they themselves worked in bronze. In Minster (Thanet) unworked metal hoards have been found with bronze swords, axes, spearheads, knives, hammers and sickles. In 1992, during excavations in Dover, waterlogged timbers of a Bronze Age boat were found. It was recovered section by section and taken away for conservation. 'The world's oldest boat', as the local newspaper recorded, was unveiled in S.E. Kent's Museum in 1999.

By 600 B.C. the settlers had learnt to work in iron. These Iron Age people were farmers as well as metal workers; and they lived in hill fort villages as a defence against their enemies. Bigbury, near Canterbury, is a hill fort with a ditch and bank for defence and an enclosure probably used as a cattle compound. There was also a metal shop where iron sickles and billhooks were made for the farming community. These people too had a religious cult. In 1971 in Broadstairs, in a new housing estate, excavators found the skeletons of a young boy and girl curled into a small circular grave dug in chalk. Nearby was a rib of beef for their future life.

Ever since Neolithic times, about 2000 B.C., people in Kent were great traders and it is interesting to notice that many of the settlements which have been discovered are on or near trading routes. The 'Pilgrims' Way' was an important west–east route via Trottiscliffe and Aylesford to Canterbury. Their second great route was the Ridgeway, following the crest of the Downs and clearly seen on Bluebell Hill, Aylesford, and cutting through the Bigbury Iron Age fort to Canterbury. They were traders in tin, gold and silver; but the local flint nodules were still a vital raw material. We have followed their trade routes by finding single coins in bronze, iron, gold or silver, or hoards of coins in hollow flints.

CHAPTER 5

Pickey Lane

THE PILGRIMS' WAY IN KENT can be followed, although sometimes
with difficulty, from Westerham to Canterbury, some 52 miles; it is
the shortest 'west-east' route across the county by country lane, by
bridle path or undefined footpath through wood or field. Elliston
Erwood, in *Archaeologia Cantiana* said: 'There is probably no other road
or trackway in the whole of England that can boast such a literature as
does this path, around which myth, legend, history, enthusiasm and
tradition have combined to weave a very tangled web.' Made famous
by Chaucer, the Way is traditionally the pilgrims' route to Canterbury.
Our minds can conjure many a colourful scene of Chaucer's pilgrims
in the 14th century, wending their way to the shrine of St. Thomas
Becket along the flint-stone road hedged in by tree and bush. In places,
below Marley Farm at Lenham, this original flint metalling can still be
seen; and today along the shady 'Way' east of Charing, one sees the
Hazel Nut, the Blackthorn and the Wayfaring tree, locally called the
Pilgrims' Tree, with its clusters of white flowers in summer and its
purplish black berries in autumn. Here and there along this bridle path
there are Yew trees, supposedly planted when a pilgrim died on his
long and tiring journey; and more happily throughout the summer the
blue Nettle-leaved Bellflower (Campanula Trachelium) blooms along
the hedgerows; popularly called the Canterbury Bell, it is believed that
this was gathered and the seeds scattered by the pilgrims while
travelling to Canterbury.

Historically such a tradition of a 'Pilgrims' Way' seems unfounded,
certainly in East Kent. These travellers would need food and rest;
there was the 'Black Horse' at Thurnham, the 'Cock' Inn at Detling
and the 'King's Head' at Hollingbourne, where today one can see
behind the inn a stone barn which would have provided rest and
shelter. Too often the villages are off the 'Way'. Boxley church and
barn, reputed to be a rest house for the pilgrims, are $^1/_4$ mile to the
south; an extra burden for many weary travellers en route to

Canterbury. The 'Way' in Kent is broken by three rivers, the Darent, Medway and Stour; it reached the Medway at Snodland and traditionalists believe that small boats plied this river to Burham Court to rejoin the 'Way'. It would seem more likely that many pilgrims would travel north to Rochester, cross the bridge and join the throng of pilgrims travelling from London, reaching Canterbury via Watling Street, along which there were numerous hostelries such as the 'Maison Dieu' at Ospringe.

The 'Way' is much older than Chaucer's pilgrims; it is thought to be a pre-historic route. In those days, 2000 B.C., when much of Kent was inhospitable and thickly wooded, Neolithic man lived, fought, worshipped and travelled on the North Downs. There is much evidence of this. Their main route east-west would have been the 'Pilgrims' Way'; it is a drychalk road built mainly along the lower slopes of the south-facing scarp of the North Downs above the Gault clay Vale of Holmesdale and below the clay-with-flints on the Ridge, which would have made travelling difficult and wet in winter. In a line from Addington to Bluebell Hill via Trottiscliffe, nowhere far from the 'Way', there are the remains of Neolithic culture; the stone circle in a farmyard at Addington, the sarsen stones in the foundations of Trottiscliffe Church and the dolmen on the slope above Aylesford.

The 'Way' was a traders' route too. Some claim that from the Bronze Age it was a pack road for tin from the mines of Cornwall to the Kent coast, whence it was shipped to the Continent. Drovers and their animals and farmers and their horse-drawn carts, would have used this road. Even after 1728, when the turnpike toll road from Maidstone to Charing was built further south, many would still follow the well known route to avoid the tax. These slopes of the North Downs provided ample chalk for quarrying and burning for lime. The 'Way' was the only route for many pits now long disused.

From exploring this route it is evident that it is a very old trackway; in places north of Godmersham it can be clearly traced as a sunken road, a deep trench bordered by high banks and we can imagine Neolithic man using this route and looking across the Stour to Juliberrie's Down, a pre-historic burial ground. Traditionally it is still a Pilgrims' Way. Perhaps from a Kentish place name we can learn the true story. The locals tell us that the lane leading to Shalmesford (east of Chilham) Manor was once called Pickey Lane; now it is Pilgrims'

Lane as it is on the line of the 'Way'. A pickeer is a 'tramp'; presumably this lane has long been the haunt of wanderers and travellers and even of traders and pilgrims.

CHAPTER 6

The Devil Upside Down

TODAY THE VILLAGE CHURCH, the city cathedral, the ruins of a monastery or friary, may well be the focus of interest for the passing traveller. In the Middle Ages, however, these were an integral part of the lives of the community.

All Englishmen were members of one Catholic Church. The parish priests were known to everyone. Many church records in Kent date back to the Middle Ages. Biddenden can list the priests since 1283 from the old account books and Barfreystone from 1259; but perhaps even more interesting was St Richard, Rector of Charing in 1243. The priest was given a house, farm buildings and a tithe, which was one tenth of every parishioner's farm and garden produce. Charing had eleven manors and records tell us that a tithe from one might consist of 'a sester of honey and three sheep; sixty loaves, twelve pence for wine and fourteen pence for ale'. From this and the offerings on feast days, the priest had to give alms to the poor, finance his household and entertain the Archbishop. The priest and the parishioners were responsible for the maintenance of the church, the building and the vestments. The Manor House by Charing Church (now Palace Farm) is often referred to as the Archbishop's Palace. We know that John Stratford, Archbishop of Canterbury 1333-48, lived there for some time and probably added the fine Gate House and the Banqueting Hall. On Sundays the priest said Matins and Mass, taught the parish children, chanted Litany and Evensong. Occasionally Miracle Plays were performed in the church or churchyard. Perhaps this is the origin of the one-time annual event of Morris dancing in Charing on Spring Bank Holiday. Only a few months ago Ashford's *Review* reported that the Borough Council and English Heritage were setting up a programme of financial aid to preserve Kent's historic buildings and the Archbishop's Palace was one of these.

The parish priests were ordained by the Bishops (Archbishops), who were elected by the Chapter of the Cathedral. Canterbury was a

Cathedral Priory financed by 63 estates, the towns and villages of the present day, such as Charing, Lenham, Sandwich and Godmersham. The Bishop and his monks were responsible for the services in the Cathedral, the daily Matins, Vespers and High Mass. There were Feast-day processions; and Miracle plays in the nave; and Canterbury soon became the centre of pilgrimages after the murder of Thomas Becket. Many pilgrims came along Watling Street from London and Stone Street from Dover. In 1420 it is recorded that 100,000 people travelled to his shrine. Visit the church at Godmersham, one of the Cathedral estates, to see the small marble wall carving of St Thomas Becket, dated around 1200.

At the time of the Norman conquest of Kent, monasteries were in decline. Lanfranc, William's chief adviser, was elected Archbishop of Canterbury. Benedictine monks from Normandy and Cistercians from Burgundy came to Kent and Lanfranc set about re-founding monasteries like Minster in Sheppey and founding new ones like Boxley Abbey (Maidstone). The daily routine of the monks was prayer, study and the successful running of the household; the refectory, the cellar, the infirmary and the garden. At their best, the monasteries gave hospitality and cheap or free lodging to travellers and food to the poor. They even founded schools and hospitals. In Kent today we can still visit some of the smaller houses built for the sick and old and to provide shelter for pilgrims. The Maison Dieu, Dover, was used by foreign pilgrims on their way to Canterbury and the people of Sandwich founded St Bartholomew's Hospital to give thanks for victory over the French on St Bartholomew's Day. It is now almshouses for the elderly. At their worst, the monasteries had little contact with the community and became retreats for the well-to-do, forgetting St Benedict and his rules of poverty and simplicity.

Because of the 'decline' of the monasteries by the beginning of the 13th century, many people were ready to welcome the Friars, when they came to England from the Continent, who were prepared to live less comfortably, often begging for their living, while at the same time preaching and teaching. Within 50 years the Dominicans (Blackfriars) and Franciscans (Greyfriars) had settled in Canterbury and the Carmelites (Whitefriars) had founded Aylesford Priory, which still plays a vital role in the Church today. But soon many friars became like Chaucer's friar, 'a wanton and a merry' who 'knew the taverns well in every town'.

In Kent today we can probably more readily recognise the importance of religion in the Middle Ages by studying the buildings of our parish churches and great cathedrals. Their structure was very strong and simple but their decoration was lavish. Examine the cool, low-pitched Norman crypt in Canterbury Cathedral, with its massive sculptured pillars and crowns of thorns in the roof; and then examine the intricate carvings of the west door. Or visit Rochester with its finely decorated west front. Go inside to see the great Norman nave and outside to sit in the peaceful ruins of the cloisters. Then there is Minster-in-Thanet with its dog-tooth moulding on the rounded Norman arch of the west door, and Dymchurch with its beautifully carved chancel arch and south

The Wall paintings, Brook Church.

doorway. Many people could not read and so it was essential that their beliefs should be illustrated for them in paintings, in stained glass, in carvings in wood and stone. Throughout Kent there is much evidence of this. In Cliffe, Brook and Capel wall paintings have long been 'preserved' under Victorian plaster, now uncovered at great cost and too often damaged. On reading this my friend remarked that his grandfather, the Revd. Harry Capel, had been the incumbent Vicar at Capel Church when the magnificent murals were found and then uncovered under the direction of Professor E. W. Tristram around 1929. Previously in 1908 he had also studied the Medieval paintings in Brook church which depict scenes in the life of Christ.

The lead font, Brookland Church.

More recently in the 1970's a 13th-century wall painting illustrating the murder of Thomas Becket was found and cleaned in Brookland church at a cost of £114. Then there are the misericords, animals and men, in Westwell; Jack-in-the-Green in Charing and the carved wooden plaque at Dymchurch representing the Resurrection and in Brookland the lead font portraying the signs of the Zodiac and the work of each month.

Above all, perhaps, Barfreystone is the symbol of the Mediaeval Church. Built of Caen stone, delivered to the craftsmen en route from Sandwich to Canterbury, it is almost as the Normans left it in the 12th century. It is simple in plan: nave and chancel in the traditional

The South Doorway, Barfreystone Church.

Norman style, semi-circular arches, thick walls and narrow slits for windows; but added to this, the skilful stone masons themselves have left their signatures (their masons' marks) and their craft. There is 12th-century stained glass in the wheel window and an enormous array of faces, religious and secular, man and animal, which smile, frown, grimace or laugh at you whichever way you turn. On the east wall we see the Eagle for St. John, the winged Bull for St. Luke and the Lion for St. Mark; but look around you for the bear playing a harp, a fox jumping for joy, a dragon chewing both its tails, dogs chasing a cat, a mason instructing an apprentice and the head of the devil upside-down.

CHAPTER 7

Smuggling[*]

IN THE MIDDLE AGES Romney Marsh was the haunt of smugglers. It was near to France and London; it was lonely, wild and unknown. It was criss-crossed by narrow winding lanes which all led to the sea, and the Marshmen loved the sea and adventure.

The Marshes, too, were the home of large flocks of sheep; their fleeces were sent to the cloth-makers in Belgium and Holland, where the finest wools were spun and woven. When Edward III needed some money, he imposed a tax on every fleece exported. Now the Marshmen soon found a means of selling their wool without paying the tax; thousands of fleeces left the shallow beaches around the Marsh when it was dark and, in return, wine, brandy, silks and laces were brought ashore. The churches at Ivychurch, Brookland, Appledore and Fairfield all made good 'hideouts' until the cargo could be distributed. The 'Woolpack' Inn, two miles out of Brookland, was one of the smugglers' haunts; ponies laden with two packs of wool (240 lbs each) went by night to meet the French tub-boats waiting on the beaches.

By the 17th century there were government officers called 'Preventive Men' who were employed to stop the smuggling trade. Their task was made impossible by the secret 'hideouts' and the unfriendly terrain of the Marshes which the smugglers knew so well. Local records describe vividly the smugglers' exploits and the skirmishes which frequently occurred along the shore between Hythe and Rye. Lydd became the centre of the trade. The gangs of smugglers, armed with musketoons and pistols, were too strong for the Preventive Men. Law and order were undermanned and the smugglers had much support within the local community. So smuggling continued well into the 19th century, when wine and brandy, silks and laces, tea and tobacco were being sold tax free in the Marsh villages. As Rudyard Kipling wrote:

---

[*]Derived from a Saxon word, 'Smugan', to creep about.

The 'Woolpack' Inn.

If you wake at midnight and hear a horse's feet,
Don't go drawing back the blind or looking in the street,
Them that asks no questions isn't told a lie . . .
   Five and twenty ponies
   Trotting through the dark –
   Brandy for the Parson,
   'Baccy for the Clerk;
   Laces for a Lady, letters for a spy. . .
If you see the stable yard sitting open wide
If you see a tired horse lying down inside;
If your Mother mends a coat cut about and tore;
If the lining's wet and warm – don't you ask no more.

CHAPTER 8

'A Great Trade in Planting of Hops'

(Taken from Harrison: *Description of England*, 1577)

'AUGUST THE 29TH 1743 began hopping and it lasted 8 days. It was fine weather to pick 'em in. My hops were very fine this year and a pretty good crop'. So reads an extract from Richard Tylden's accounts of his farm at Milstead.

By the eighteenth century hops were an established part of the Kentish landscape. Ale had been brewed at least as early as the twelfth century, but bitter beer was first made in the sixteenth century when 'the hoppe' was introduced by the Flemish weavers, many of whom settled in the Weald of Kent. It is interesting to note that records of the cloth industry tell us that the last product of the Cranbrook looms and shuttles in 1860 was 'a coarse kind of stuff called hop bagging, being a kind of rough linen cloth'.

Hop growing has always been an expensive industry, but Kent had many local advantages. Farms were enclosed and a yeoman farmer owned perhaps 200 acres of cereals and pasture. Now he introduced a half- or one-acre hop garden to provide a cash crop. However, by 1604 George Franklin had 16 acres on the crest of the ragstone ridge at Chart Sutton. The natural advantages of hill slopes and valleys, of clay sand soils and of cold winters and sunny summers with a dry autumn season for harvesting, encouraged the farmer and yet there was still the risk of total loss in poor weather. In 1695 at St Mary's Cray, there were no hops, 'they being all blacked' by the weather and next year 'blacked and spoyled with the blast'. Hops needed to be protected by 'lews', which were hawthorn hedges 12-15 feet high or wild hops on close set poles or coarse canvas stretched from pole to pole along the whole of the windward side of the garden. This is still evident in Kent's remaining hop-growing regions today.

Local wood, mainly ash and chestnut, was cut for hop poles. Right up until the end of the nineteenth century there were three poles to each hill, which had to be renewed frequently. John Evelyn, the diarist, conducted an anti-hop campaign against cutting down young trees for poles. Today fewer poles are used. They were replaced first by an intricate pattern of strings and then by overhead wire and strings for training the bines.

The local timber supplied the charcoal for drying the hops. At first, in the sixteenth century, hops were dried in the attic but soon the oast house was built. Then a hop-dryer was employed like Goodman Dutnal at Milstead in 1743, who earned 16/- for drying hops for eight days. The early oasts were rectangular barns with storage space at each end for undried and dried hops, and with one or more kilns in the middle. This centre room was 8 feet square with a drying rack 5 feet above the ground. The small brick furnace 13 inches wide and deep by 6 feet long had regularly shaped holes on the sides to allow the heat from the charcoal to rise through the 1½-feet thick bed of hops on the rack above. These kilns gave way in the nineteenth century to the traditional Kentish oast house with its round or square kiln, its picturesque tall roof and cowl attached to an adjoining storage building.

Local materials were used for the buildings such as the timber and stone built and thatched oast house with 8 square kilns recorded at Binbury Farm, Thurnham, in 1859. Visit Pluckley today, where six round oasts are preserved with Kentish ragstone walls, Bethersden marble floors, an old kiln and cowls decorated with the Black Horse of the local Dering family. Oasts with ragstone and flint, bricks, tiles and slates, and often with weather-boarded storage buildings, are reminiscent of the past. Too many are disappearing through neglect. Others are converted into homes and no more will be built now that the hops are dried more efficiently with hot air circulated by electric fans, so that the tall roof and cowl are now a tradition rather than a necessity.

Kent had the advantage of being accessible to large supplies of seasonal labour. By the mid-seventeenth century, 'hoppers' from London were travelling to Kent in the autumn at harvest time. As Celia Fiennes wrote in 1697 about her journey from Maidstone to Rochester, 'I came by a great many hopp yards where they were at work pulling the hopps'. There were the hoppers who picked into the bins; the pole-pullers who fetched the hop-bines for them and the bin

Oast houses, Sheerland, Pluckley.

men who measured the hops. As Richard Tylden's accounts record, 'Old Goody Marten and Betty Marten at one end of the bin and Goody Court at the other end'. John Middleton and Daniel Kemp were bin men and earnt 12/- at 1/6d per day for eight days, wet or dry, and James Croyden sometimes fetched the hops. 'Hopping' has progressed from hand-picking into canvas bins to harvesting by machines, which strip the bines, blow away the leaves, and pass the hops along a conveyor belt to half a dozen women who snatch any large bunches and leaves which may spoil 'the sample'.

Today the elderly are frequently heard to remark on a bright, frosty autumn morning, 'It's a hoppicking (hopping) morning' as they recall the comradeship of friends and the 'pin money' earnt to feed and clothe a growing family.

Finally, Kent was in an ideal position for trade in hops, for London was a ready market where brewing developed early. Franklin of Chart Sutton was sending hops to the City of London through the port of Rochester as early as 1598. Now, approaching the Millennium, with increasing and easier international trade and the specialist demands of the brewers, Kent's growing of, and trading in, 'the hoppe' has declined dramatically. Only last year I met a farmer in Smarden who had been forced to allow half a garden to blow away. Yet 'hoppes' and hopping, oasts both round and square, are traditional to Kent and have been an important part of the Kentish landscape in all seasons of the year. 'Shoe money' is no longer collected to pay for the feast of bread, cheese and ale when hopping is over. Yet the hop bine is still seen in local churches at harvest festivals and hanging in the bar in many Kentish pubs. The pungent smell of kiln-drying hops is rare in the Kent countryside today, but as Dickens said, 'Kent, Sir – everybody knows Kent . . . Apples, cherries, hops and women'.

CHAPTER 9

'Plum Pottage and Nativity Pies'

'S TONE WALLS DO NOT A PRISON MAKE – Nor iron bars a cage'. So wrote Richard Lovelace. In St Margaret's Church at Bethersden it is easy to conjure up a picture of the gallant young Richard, poet and Royalist. His portrait often looks at us out of the local history book in the showcase; on the wall are the brasses in memory of his family, whose home was 'Lovelace', half a mile to the west. Bethersden parish records tell us that at the beginning of the 19th century this house was derelict and William Baldwin built Lovelace Place a few yards away. A small executive housing estate, Lovelace Court, has now been built on the original site. In 1642 Richard was imprisoned, when along with 200 Kentish gentlemen he handed a petition to Parliament requesting that 'a good understanding be come to between King and Parliament so that a law be framed for the regulating of the Militia of the King so that the subjects may know how at once to obey both His Majesty and the Houses of Parliament.'

There were numerous grievances. The payment of taxes was unpopular; Charles I was attempting to raise money by dubious means. In 1626 the King asked for 'loans' and Kent's loan was fixed at £6,711. In 1635 he made a country-wide demand for 'ship-money'. In Kent it was to be paid by instalments over 5 years to a total of nearly £35,000. By 1640 Kent was asked to assemble 1,000 men and provide £1,750 to support them. And in various parts of Kent, especially in the Weald, where non-conformity was growing, the people resented Archbishop Laud's efforts to reform the Church (in Anglo-Catholic times). Petitions were prepared setting out these grievances, for Kentish gentlemen were neither Royalist nor Parliamentarian. Men like Sir John Culpeper of Leeds Castle and Sir Edward Dering of Surrenden-Dering, Pluckley, were responsible for delivering the documents to Westminster.

When the Civil War broke out in August 1642, few Kentish gentlemen sent support to the King but amongst those who did were Sir Edward Dering, Sir John Culpeper, Sir William Clark of

Dering windows, Pluckley.

Hollingbourne and Richard Thornhill of Olantigh, Wye. These were county gentlemen and held large estates. The estate of Sir Edward Dering can easily be traced today, centred in the picturesque village of Pluckley with its Kentish ragstone cottages with their round, arched windows. The story is told that one of Sir Edward's family escaped by night from the Parliamentarians by climbing through such a window. Once the war started, there was fighting in Kent.

Parliamentarian soldiers made skirmishes attacking the homes of Royalist supporters and the castles of Rochester, Dover, Deal, Walmer and Sandown were taken without resistance. The altar rails were smashed in Rochester Cathedral and medieval stained glass was destroyed in Canterbury. The first street fighting was at Ightham, where the vicar had refused to make his parishioners swear allegiance to the Parliamentarian forces. They fought and lost. Parliament was gaining control.

Some of the fiercest fighting of the Civil War was at Canterbury. Records tell us that here, in 1647, Christmas festivities were made illegal. Church services were banned, shops would be kept open, and there was to be no making of 'plum pottage and nativity pies', 'no hanging of holly, rosemary or bay at the street door'. In Canterbury this was ignored. The Mayor was attacked in the street whilst trying to persuade traders to open their shops, but they rioted. By the end of January the Parliamentarians had captured the city and the County Committee which ruled Kent became extreme. The rioters filed a petition asking that they might be governed by the 'established laws of the Kingdom'. This was refused. Now Royalists and Parliamentarians met in Maidstone. The Royalists gathered on Penenden Heath, guarded the river crossings at Aylesford and Maidstone, and also guarded the North Downs approach at Kits Coty. The Parliamentarians crossed the Medway at Barming and Farleigh in the south. They met on Gabriel's Hill, where today the narrow street links the north of the town to the south. Historical records tell us that 'every object of the town was got by inches', and the Royalists finally surrendered at midnight.

Kent was involved in this struggle between the King and his Parliament until the final moment, even to the execution of Charles I on 30th January, 1649. Andrew Broughton, an attorney of Earl Street, Maidstone, was the Clerk of the Court which sentenced the King. And yet, perhaps, Kent gained something from this war: the poetry of the imprisoned Richard Lovelace and the altar cloth attributed to the daughters of Sir Thomas Culpeper of Hollingbourne and said to have been embroidered by them while he was away fighting for the King. The rich purple velvet pall was beautifully worked in fine gold thread, and illustrates the Kentish fruits: grapes, apples, pears, cherries, plums and cobnuts. It is extremely valuable and may be seen on request to the Vicar.

CHAPTER 10

Damson Broadcloth

Between 1400 and 1700 Kent was a prosperous cloth-making county. A yard of damson-coloured broadcloth or wool cloth would cost about 50p, a labourer's wage for a fortnight. In Biddenden, Canterbury, Cranbrook, Sandwich and Smarden there is much evidence of the wealth of Kentish clothiers and merchants. There are the cloth halls. Besides being the home of the clothier, these halls contained workshops for the weavers and sometimes dyeing vats, and were used as the collecting place for all the cloth made in the villages. They reflect the prosperity of their owners; most are fine buildings with tall chimneys, leaden windows, gables, half-timbered and tile-hung walls, and occasionally there is evidence of the hoist used for unloading the bales of wool. The Cloth Hall in Smarden is a fine example.

Many smaller houses in these villages and towns were the homes of the cloth workers, where the wool was carded and spun; and the Dutch gables seen in some of them remind us of the foreign influence on the industry. Edward III first encouraged craftsmen from Holland, Belgium and France to settle in this country and practise their skills. Many came to Kent and were often called 'Strangers' because they spoke their own language and followed their native customs. By 1694 in Canterbury, there were 2,700 such 'strangers' working 1,000 looms and making serges, taffetas, ribbons, laces and fringes of wool and silk. In those days the River Stour looked gay with the red-sailed barges from the Continent, loaded with bales of raw wool and raw silk on the way to Canterbury. In Cranbrook and Biddenden, on the other hand, the pack horses would be seen travelling along the rough, unmade roads with their bales of raw wool.

Much was bought from local Wealden farmers. It is recorded that in 1632 Thomas Couchman of Pluckley bought 17 quarters from Thomas Waterman of Bethersden. After the wool had been spun and woven, the broadcloth had to be cleaned and brushed. Cleaning (or fulling)

The Cloth Hall, Smarden.

was done in huge troughs of water containing a grey soil called Fullers' earth, which was to be found locally. In Kent most clothiers dyed their yarn before weaving and became famous for their great variety of colours to make 'medley' cloths. In 1601 Alexander Sheafe of Cranbrook was making 'black and white grey cloths', 'olive and grey cloths', 'black, red and green', and 'brown and blue'. Documents show that in 1627 William Allen, also of Cranbrook, had 'red wood galls and other dyeing stuff' in his work house.

When there was inadequate water in Wealden streams, the cloth was taken to fulling mills along the River Len and the Loose Stream, near to the main supply of Fullers' earth at Boxley near Maidstone. The fullers walked on it, but at Turkey Mill on the River Len the water was sufficient both for fulling and for power to pound the broadcloth with hammers. Finally the broadcloth was stretched on wooden frames called tenters and brushed with teazles, collected from river banks, to draw up the loose threads. These were snipped off by the shearman.

Each piece of broadcloth was officially inspected to make sure that it had not been stretched too much on the tenters or cut too closely by the shearman. A 'piece' was 1³/₄ yards in breadth and 30 yards in

The Weavers' houses, Canterbury.

length. This too had to be checked to make sure that it weighed 66 lbs. Such a 'piece' would sell at approximately £12.00 undyed. A damson-coloured broadcloth would cost £16.00 or more.

CHAPTER 11

'A Very Queer Small Boy'

'Holloa!' said I to the 'very queer small boy', 'Where do you live?'
'At Chatham,' says he.
'What do you do there?, says I.
'I go to school,' says he.
Presently the very queer small boy said: 'This is Gadshill. We are coming to where Falstaff went out to rob those travellers and then ran away... I am old, I am nine and I read all sorts of books.'
'You admire that house?' said I.
'Bless you, Sir,' said the very queer small boy, 'Ever since I can recollect, my father has often said to me: 'If you were to be very persevering and were to work hard, you might some day come to live in it.'
This is a fragment of autobiography in *The Uncommercial Traveller*, written in 1861, and 'the very queer small boy' was Charles Dickens. His father joined the Navy, so Dickens spent his childhood in Chatham, living in 'a tenement with a plain-looking whitewashed front' and his writings vividly reflect his memories of the people and the landscape. Chatham was 'a mere dream of chalk and drawbridge and mastless ships in a muddy river', and 'Marine stones, hardbake, apples, flatfish and oysters' were sold in the streets.
In 1822 Dickens left for London in a stage coach. He records: 'I have never lost the smell of the damp straw in which I was packed like game and forwarded, carriage paid, to the "Cross Keys", Cheapside, London.' Today it is easy to re-people Chatham with Dickensian characters from *David Copperfield*, *Great Expectations* and *The Pickwick Papers*.
In 1856 the ambition of 'the very queer small boy' was realised when he bought Gads Hill Place, for £1,790. Many of Dickens' later novels were written in a Swiss chalet in his garden at Gads Hill, from which he could see the Cooling Marshes. It is these which he described so vividly in *Great Expectations* as a '... dark, flat wilderness

beyond the churchyard, intersected with dykes and mounds and gates, with scattered cattle feeding on it.' It is in Cooling churchyard, too, where he describes the five miniature graves of Pip's young brothers, Alexander, Bartholomew, Abraham, Tobias and Roger in *The Pickwick Papers*. Visiting the Cooling Marshes one winter afternoon, we found the tiny graves at the foot of the churchyard wall as described by Dickens and it was easy to share the terror experienced by Pip at the sudden appearance of the convict.

Dickens is said to have enjoyed walking to Maidstone. To him it was 'one of the most beautiful walks in England'. Perhaps he found Dingley Dell and the pond, and even met the characters of Mr Winkle and Sam Weller somewhere en route. It is recorded that throughout his life Dickens loved to disguise himself so that he could mingle with the people in the streets, getting inspiration for his novels So it is easy to imagine the Kent of his day. Visit Canterbury and there is Mr Wickfield's house in the High Street, '. . . a very old house bulging out over the road, with long low lattice windows bulging out still further, so that I fancied the whole house was leaning forward trying to see who was passing on the narrow pavement below'. Then in Castle Street there is the 'mean house of Uriah Heep, the low, old-fashioned room entered straight from the street'.

In *The Pickwick Papers* Dickens portrays the Rochester of his day. He describes '. . . its frowning walls, tottering arches, dark nooks, crumbling staircases and little Saxon doors'. He sent Pip '. . . to bed in the attic with a sloping roof which was so low in the corner where the bedstead was that I [Pip] calculated the tiles as being within a foot of my eyebrows'.

At Dickens' death in 1870, Longfellow said: 'Dickens was so full of life that it did not seem possible he could die'. The Kentish towns, people and landscape of his day still live through his writings. Perhaps even the 'hostelries' frequented by Dickensian characters, such as the 'Fountain' hotel where Mr Dick stayed, the 'little inn', the 'Sun', where Mr Micawber gave David his 'choice dinner' and the 'Leather Bottle' Inn patronised by Mr Tracy Tupman retain some of the 19th-century flavour portrayed for us so vividly through the inspiration of 'a very queer small boy'.

The 'Sun' Inn, Canterbury, where Mr Micawber gave David his 'choice dinner'.

CHAPTER 12

L. Munn, Kent 1809

HISTORY RECORDS THAT IN 1588 John Spilman leased two watermills on the Darenth at Dartford and was given 'the monopoly of the making of white paper' for the next ten years. He was authorised to 'gather all manner of linen rags, scraps of parchment, leather shreds, clippings of cards and old fishing nets necessary for the making of white paper'. Six hundred skilled vatmen were employed in Spilman's mills. Other mills were opened at Eynsford, Buckland (Dover), Canterbury, and before 1700 seven mills were making paper in the Medway valley within two to three miles of Maidstone. One of these was in Mill Street, Maidstone and another very small one was at Aylesford, within a few hundred yards of the present mill, built by Albert E. Reed and Company Ltd. in the early 1900's. It is recorded that in 1696 Thomas Hatton of Buckland Mill had in 'ye ragghouse 23 cwt. of paper stuffe, stuffe ready beaten to make 21 reams of paper and one ream of paper a-drying in ye lodge' and by 1700 'over 3,000 reams of paper, 80 tons of pasteboard, parchment and brown paper were being shipped to London from Rochester, Faversham and Dover.

Kent had a leading role in the paper products industry as early as the 16th and 17th centuries, when the sites had been chosen along the valleys of the Darenth, Medway, Len, Loose and the Stour. Water was, and still is, a vital raw material. Originally plenty of pure, clear water was needed for cleaning and pulping the linen rags and in the actual paper-making process for settling the fibres. Pure spring water from Mote Park was used at Turkey Mill on the River Len and water pumped from the Greensands supplied Ford Mill, Little Chart. Water for power, clear and cheap, was equally important. The rivers were pounded back into reservoirs for water storage. Many corn and fulling mills became paper mills: Turkey Mill was converted from fulling to paper in 1690; the hammers formerly used for pounding cloth were now used for making paper and board. In 1739 the mill was rebuilt.

Owned by the Whatman family, it soon became the largest paper mill in England. Whatman and Turkey Mill paper were synonymous.

Kent had other incentives for a flourishing paper industry. Rag was an essential ingredient. The earliest paper was brown, made of old ropes and sails from Kentish ports. Spilman began to make white paper. London was the chief source of woollen and linen rags. In 1719, in his *History of Kent*, Harris says that the good white paper made in a mill on the Len near Maidstone was produced partly from London rags. Then rags from France and Belgium as well as from London supplied Turkey Mill. Huge bales of cotton and linen rags were always evident in the 'ragghouse'.

London was not only the main source of rag fibres, but also the market for finished paper. The chief incentive to this industry was Kent's proximity to London. The Medway was navigable. Rochester, Faversham and Dover were flourishing trading ports. Fleet Street was already the centre of the newspaper world. In 1861 the excise duty on paper was abolished and paper-making expanded. At the end of the century the ½d newspaper was introduced.

Gradually during the 20th century the character of much of the industry has changed. Large mills grew on the river banks below Maidstone at Aylesford, and further downstream at Sittingbourne and Kemsley. Barges plied the Medway loaded with foreign wood pulp and china clay from Cornwall for the large mills making newsprint, tissues, sacks, corrugated paper and pipes. Bowater Scott had its own company dock at Ridham on the Swale. Yet lorry loads of waste paper and rags continued to reach the old-established specialist mills making high-quality paper.

Whilst visiting Ford Mill, Little Chart, it was interesting to learn that a sheet of hand-made paper watermarked 'L. Munn, Kent, 1809' had been discovered during alteration work. Records tell us that Munn established a 'one-vat' paper mill here in 1776, on the site of a corn-grinding mill. In the middle of the 19th century it was taken over by Joseph Batchelor, who established a flourishing business making hand-made paper using Stour water, stored in a giant pond, for processing and for power. For three generations fine white paper continued to be made until 1944. With the growth of the newspaper trade demand changed, and with the speedier and cheaper production of machine-made paper in the large Medway mills, Ford Mill began to produce stereo-flong for the printing trade and the 'ragghouse' became the store for old cheques and computer cards, which were the raw fibres for making its new product. Today, in the 21st c., lorry loads of ready-made paper (from home and abroad) arrive at Ford Mill to be cut, trimmed, packaged and marketed at home and abroad.

CHAPTER 13

More than Five Hundred Years of History

I N 1944 THE EDUCATION ACT made it the duty of the Kent
Education Authority 'to contribute towards the spiritual, moral,
mental and physical development of the community by securing that
efficient education, throughout three progressive stages – primary,
secondary and further education shall be available to meet the needs of
the population' of the county. Great strides had been made in the
growth of education during the 18th and 19th centuries, but in 1944
national statistics showed that secondary education was available for
only 9.5% of the children eligible by age, although every Kent parish
had an elementary school.

Travelling through the picturesque village of Wye today, one might
scarcely notice the small one-storey, flint and ragstone building in the
corner of the churchyard. Known as the 'Latin' school, it was founded
by John Kempe, Archbishop of York, in 1447, along with Wye College,
a residence for secular priests. It was, in fact, one of three monastic
schools in pre-Reformation Kent. With the suppression of the
monasteries in 1538, King's School, Canterbury was put under the
control of the Dean and Chapter, as a part of Henry's Reformation
settlement, to teach fifty poor boys Latin and Greek. Apart from this,
we hear little of the Church's influence in education until the early
19th century, when many elementary schools were built under its
auspices. It was often due to the enthusiasm and energy of the local
vicar and was indicative of the interest being taken in the welfare of
the poor. Brookland village school is a good example. It was first held
in the church porch and then in the vestry, and the vicar was the
schoolmaster. By 1800 there were 50 pupils and 70 years later the
present school was built with the help of the Church of England
Society, 'The National Society for the Promotion of the Education of
the Poor'. The school log book makes fascinating reading:

'The Reverend Baldock visited the school and heard a lesson on the
Ball Frame.'

The Latin School, Wye College.

'Two children absent through harvesting.'

'Not so large a school this week as many of the children are at work cutting wurzels.'

'Three children kept away to gather wool.'

'Several children away hop picking.'

It is still a Church of England school, although controlled by the state. Ightham village school too was built in 1815 under the auspices of the Church of England Society. Its aim was that 'children be taught reading and writing' and the girls in addition 'the use of the needle and knitting'. To learn reading and writing cost 2d per head per week but 1d only to learn to read. Other schools, particularly in towns, were founded by 'The British and Foreign Schools Society', a non-conformist group. Bethany School, Goudhurst, opened in 1866 by the Reverend J. Kendon, a Baptist Minister, is still independent and prides itself on its religious foundation. *The Wealden Advertiser*, 25th February 2000, advertises it as 'A happy, thriving school community which is refreshingly different'.

'The use of the needle and knitting' at Ightham village school must be one of the first references made to teaching girls in school. Right up until the early 19th century education for girls was at home. We can learn much from contemporary novelists such as Jane Austen. Her heroines were all accomplished 'young ladies' learning to sing, draw, dance, play the piano or harp, 'to write a good hand and listen to the gentlemen talk', and 'to indulge in housewifery and morning calls'. But an academic education was unimportant. So it is the more interesting to note in Kent the foundation of a girls' school in 1835. We read '5 little girls sitting on 5 wooden stools made especially for them' were present at the opening meeting of the 'School and Home for Missionaries' Daughters' at Walthamstow. A few friends founded Walthamstow Hall (now in Sevenoaks) 'to provide for the daughters of Christian Missionaries a thoroughly good and liberal education'. But girls had to wait until the first decade of the 20th century before secondary education was provided in most towns. Ashford, Bromley, Dover, Folkestone and Ramsgate Girls' Grammar schools were built between 1904 and 1914.

From early times, Grammar Schools provided education for the boys of the family, preparing them for the Church, for university and for a professional training in law or medicine. Wealthy benefactors endowed these schools. William Sevenoke was the first. When he died in 1432, he endowed Sevenoaks school, a free Grammar School 'for the education of boys in Latin and Greek'. The Elizabethans continued to promote a classical education. In 1638 Sir Norton Knatchbull endowed the original Ashford Grammar School, situated by the church. It still has its classroom with two masters' seats and an array of pigeonholes for books.

Latin and Greek were taught free. English and Mathematics were often taught to less able children for a small fee. At the same time elementary schools were being endowed to teach girls and boys 'to read and write and to do accounts' with knitting and needlework for the girls. Over the school door in Hothfield the inscription reads: 'The schools were erected by the Earl of Thanet in 1834, Hothfield Place.' By 1870, although 170 rural parishes had a school, there was a need for the State to provide education. School Boards were set up and attendance was for children aged between five and thirteen years. In 1891 education was made free. In 1902 the Kent Education Committee was set up to look after 'elementary and higher education' throughout the county. Since then education in Kent has seen many changes and much progress has been made towards providing the resources for educational opportunities for all, rich and poor alike, in literary, scientific and technological skills. Standards of performance of pupils and teachers are monitored by Government Officers. Today in Kent, County Primary, High School, Grammar and Comprehensive, Private, Endowed, and Public schools are names familiar to us all. But what of their history? As in the past, the Church, wealthy benefactors as well as the State all share in the continued growth of our present education system and contribute towards 'the spiritual, moral, mental and physical development of the community'.

CHAPTER 14

A Perfect Patchwork

WHETHER WE ARE IN town or village, on the Downs or in the Weald, Kentish houses are fascinating. They have 'grown up' through the centuries from Norman times to the present day and form a living record of our history.

Our houses reflect the characteristics of the generations which built them. Most of us can be delighted by the Medieval Manors of Luddesdown Court and Old Soar, Plaxtol, by the fifteenth-century Hall House at Hollingbourne, the Georgian town houses in Cranbrook, the Regency terraces in Ramsgate and even the twentieth-century architecture of New Ash Green. Domestic architecture was a craft for the carpenter, thatcher, tiler, the stonemason and bricklayer. Each dwelling is steeped in history.

Our nearness to the continent has influenced us from early times. In the eleventh century the Normans came as invaders and settled here. They brought their building skills and their craftsmen and soon introduced the famous Caen stone, so prominent in Kent. Durable and hard, Caen stone is easily carved. With additions through the centuries, Luddesdown Court still stands in its superb Downland setting. The massive rubble-filled flint walls with Caen stone coigns and doorways, have stood the test of time. The Great Hall and Solar are even now used by the present family. On the other hand, Old Soar, owned by the National Trust and preserved by the Department of the Environment, is open to the public. The Great Hall, with its steep, pitched roof, its tie beam and king post, is well worth a visit. By the sixteenth century the Dutch were coming to Kent as refugees. They settled in a 'foreign' land, living in 'colonies' and practising their art of spinning and weaving. In 1565 in Sandwich alone there were one hundred and twenty-nine 'foreign' families and their influence can be seen today in the building styles of the town. Walk along the narrow streets and you will notice the crow-stepped gables of Manwood Court and the White Friars, and the decorative house at No. 62 King Street, called 'The

Luddesdown Court.

Dutch House'. Their ideas filtered further into Kent and the typical Dutch brickwork can be seen in many villages and towns. Beacon House, Bethersden, is a handsome example. But perhaps the greatest example is the original Godinton House, Hothfield, built in 1628 in brick with mullioned windows and gables. In the seventeenth century our domestic architecture began to be influenced by the Italian Renaissance. Inigo Jones studied in Venice and Rome. Its key notes were symmetry and simplicity. Lees Court, Sheldwich, built in 1645, is a superb example, with its long front, symmetrical bays, wide overhanging eaves and Ionic pillars. Similar features attributed to Inigo Jones himself or to his pupils can be seen at Chilham, Chevening and Groombridge Place. Cobham Hall too illustrates both the Dutch influence and the classical influence of Inigo Jones.

Kent's architecture too has been affected by its nearness to London. By Elizabethan times, West Kent in particular was becoming a retreat within easy reach of London for the court and courtiers, merchants and City Aldermen. Penshurst Place originated in the fourteenth century as the country house of a city merchant and four times Lord Mayor of London, Sir John de Poulteney, who acquired a licence to fortify the house and built the Great Hall with its Minstrels' Gallery. In the 16th century it became the home of Sir Philip Sidney of literary fame. Brasted Place was the country home of John Tufton, court physician to George III. '1591' inscribed on the dining-room ceiling dates Lancelot Bathurst's house, Franks, in Horton Kirby. He was an Alderman of London and a member of the Company of Merchant Adventurers and Grocers.

Our homes were also influenced by the wealth of the Church, of the yeoman farmers, of the ironmasters and clothiers. The present Jacobean mansion at Knole was once a Medieval Palace for the Archbishop of Canterbury. The Church in the Middle Ages owned much land and throughout the county the remains of other palaces exist such as Charing, Maidstone, Wrotham and Otford. Milner Court, Sturry, belonged to St. Augustine's, Canterbury. It served as a retreat for the Abbot, with hunting and fishing, and the tithe barn reminds us of its monastic ownership. Northbourne Court was another Abbot's Grange. With the Reformation, there came a change in social conditions; wealth was now directed to domestic architecture instead of to the Church. Old houses were enlarged or pulled down and rebuilt and new houses were built out of materials taken from deserted monasteries. It was the age of culture, of music and dancing, of Flemish and Renaissance influence in many great country houses. The yeoman farmers were increasing their wealth and many of their Hall Houses remain for our delight. Traditionally timber-framed, they have two storeys at either end with a lofty hall in the centre. A tie beam inside the hall supports the king post, with its curved capital and moulded base. Many have been altered over the years but their basic plan remains the same and is easy to recognise. There is Eyhorne Manor, Hollingbourne and Old Hall, Sundridge. Iron masters and clothiers were wealthy too. Sir Edward Filmer, an ironmaster, lived in the red brick house in East Sutton Park and Wilsley House, Cranbrook was probably built by a master weaver in Tudor times and owned by John Weston, a clothier, in the seventeenth century. Larger than a Hall House, it is interesting with its two gables, Gothic barge boards, wood mullions and its Great Hall, now three storeys.

Perhaps above all it is the building materials which make Kent's domestic architecture so fascinating and full of variety, a patchwork of colour, of texture and of design. Whether in Downland, in the valleys

St. Peter's Cottage, Bethersden. End-of-terrace timber-framed cottage, originally weatherboarded on the front and tile hung in Kent peg on the end elevation.

or on the weald, in town or country, local materials are evident and there is no conformity of use in one district or one period. Walk through 'The Street' in Biddenden or Smarden, Bethersden or Lenham, Ightham or Hollingbourne, to appreciate this variety. There are dull-red Kentish tiles and bricks mellowed with age; freshly painted white clapperboards, dark Wealden oak beams and pale colour-washed plaster and stones – grey, black flints, nut-brown ironstones and light brown sandstones, all blending to a perfect whole. By the end of the nineteenth century there was a tendency for local styles and the use of local materials to disappear with the increased use of mass-produced materials and mass-produced designs. The Victorian terraces and twentieth-century Council and private estates and the 'bungalow towns' are all evidence of this and we do not have to look far for the manufacturers of these modern building materials.

CHAPTER 15

The Ruined Tower

TO THE OBSERVANT TRAVELLER in Kent today, there are constant reminders of two World Wars. Read the tiny bronze plaque in Tonbridge High Street: 'Above this roof The Battle of Britain was fought and won August 8–Oct 10 1940'. Visit the attractive village of Northiam and note the inscription: 'These gates were erected by the parishioners of Northiam to commemorate the visit of four Prime Ministers to these fields on the 12 May 1944 – Sir Winston Churchill, The Rt. Hon. Mackenzie King, The Rt. Hon. Field Marshall Jan Christian Smuts and The Rt. Hon. Sir Godfrey Higgins'. Or just look at the solidly built brick 'shed' set deeply in the backyard; the irregular hole in the neighbour's pasture; the huge concrete blocks which still litter the coastal marshes at Richborough; the Dover Patrol memorial on the White Cliffs near St. Margaret's Bay; the Zeebrugge bell on the façade of Dover Town Hall; the remains of the sites of Royal Observer Corps lookout posts or the inconspicuous war memorials in every village street. All these are reminders of Kent's part in two World Wars.

Once again, as throughout her history, Kent was in a vulnerable position. In 1216, Hubert de Burgh declared Dover to be 'the very key and gate of England'. In 1914 and again in 1939 Kent was open to foreign invasion and attack across the narrow Channel strait and was forced to set up lines of defence. In 1909 Dover Harbour, then the largest artificial harbour in the world, was opened by the Prince of Wales (later George V), and in 1914 it became the headquarters of the Dover Patrol, responsible for maintaining a safe passage across the strait for millions of men going to and from the battlefields of France and Belgium. The harbour was crowded with ships: destroyers, cruisers, submarines and supply ships. Every convoy was guarded by the Dover Patrol. By this time German submarines, from Belgian ports, were trying to cut off our food supplies. The Dover Patrol sank old cruisers, by filling them with cement, as blockships in Zeebrugge Harbour and at Ostend to stop the movement of submarines. The Zeebrugge bell, now in Dover and rung each year on St. George's Day in honour of the Dover Patrol, was once rung by the Germans to warn of British attack.

Dover too, became the focal point of World War II in 1940, when Dover Castle became the naval headquarters for the evacuation of Dunkirk – 224,000 men were brought from the French beaches in naval vessels or small craft. Coastal paddle steamers, lifeboats, yachts and motor launches landed them at Dover, Folkestone, Margate and Ramsgate.

All Kentish beaches were out of bounds throughout the Wars; barricaded with hundreds of miles of steel tubing and barbed wire, festooned with mines, and littered with huge concrete blocks to prevent an enemy landing. The Isle of Thanet, the mouth of the River Stour and the marshes at Richborough, became a 'Prohibited Area'. In World War I Ramsgate was a naval base. The fish market was a naval magazine with shells, machine guns and mines. The Smugglers' caves in the cliffs at Ramsgate were made into air-raid shelters. Nearby in 1916 the Royal Engineers were deepening and widening the River Stour and reclaiming swamp land; Stonar Cut was built to control the tide and a mile of modern wharves was built, equipped with cranes for loading war materials and train ferries for troops for France. In 1939 Richborough Port was used to build the sections of the Mulberry Harbour and the concrete pontoons which were floated to Arromanches (Normandy) then filled with water and sunk for landing equipment and troops. One can be seen today offshore at Great Stone.

The people of Kent were to play a major role in the country's battle against invasion and attack. The small ships at Dunkirk were manned by volunteers; the 'evacuees' were taken inland by train to stations where villagers worked day and night to feed them. Then there was the Home Guard on duty or on call, the Rescue-squads, Nursing and Ambulance brigades and the Air Raid wardens, as Kent was very vulnerable to air attack. Throughout the Second World War the Royal Observer Corps were in constant vigil from vantage points, such as Aldington Knoll or High Field. Bethersden, or even just a neighbour's field, scanning the sky for the approach of aircraft, squadrons of Spitfires and Hurricanes or the enemy bombers. During the Battle of Britain in the Autumn of 1940, the Germans attacked shipping in the Straits of Dover and the RAF stations throughout Kent – Biggin Hill,

Detling, Lympne and Rochester. The German Air Force invaded on September 15th – Battle of Britain Sunday; but Hitler's invasion failed. Even by 1944 Kent was still 'Bomb Alley'; first the 'Doodlebug' or V1 and then the V2 rockets were aimed at London from elaborate rocket sites on the continent. Many were brought down over Kent by the RAF or by Ack-Ack fire and finally by a Balloon Barrage. The final plans for D-Day were made in Kent.

After 1945 there remained the devastation of a major war. Some semblance of order soon returned to the Kentish countryside. The beaches were open for holiday makers; sign posts and milestones were re-erected in towns and villages; concrete obstacles were removed from cricket pitches and village greens. The ruins of the City of Canterbury around the Cathedral have been replaced by modern 'squares' and shopping façades; but the ruined 'tower' of St. Mary's Church Little Chart stands erect among the apple trees and oast houses as a daily reminder of the enemy 'doodlebug'.

CHAPTER 16

'The Splendour of God'

'SEE, SEIGNEURS, BY THE SPLENDOUR OF GOD! I have seized England with my two hands' cried Duke William as he stumbled onto the beach near Hastings. The Chronicler Master Wace records clearly and vividly the events of the Norman conquest: 'The ships were drawn to shore and the Duke landed first, he fell by chance upon his two hands. All raised a cry of distress, "an evil sign!"' But to William this was an omen of a successful conquest. The Normans' ancestors were Saxons and Vikings; they were Norsemen who had invaded Normandy in A.D. 912 and had settled there. The Norman barons were strong and powerful, but as soon as William knew that the English King Edward had died and Harold had not kept the oath that he (William) should be King of England, he prepared to invade. The Normandy Vikings had a great spirit of adventure and these were the Normans who landed at Hastings in 1066. William had planned his invasion well to avoid the Kent coast with its line of forts, Dover, Lympne, Folkestone, Richborough and Reculver. He sailed to Hastings, which was much less well defended, with nearly 700 ships, with boats for carrying arms and harness; there was a lantern on the mast of the Duke's ship so that all others would see it and hold their course for England.

'All (the Normans)', says Wace, 'were shaven and shorn and all clad in short garments ready to attack, to shoot, to wheel about and skirmish'; there were the knights with their war horses, the barons, the archers with their bows and arrows and the carpenters with their axes and planes; all were armed with shields and helmets, swords and lances.'

William gathered his forces and built a Motte-and-Bailey Castle on the East Hill to house a garrison to safeguard his fleet while he marched his army 12 miles to Pevensey where there was already a Roman fort. Much of the Roman wall with its bastions is still there today so it must have been a good stronghold for William. The historic battle on 14th October between Duke William and King Harold was fought on a low hill where Battle Abbey stands today. The English fled to London after King Harold had been killed; William did not follow. He now marched his archers, infantry and knights eastward along the coast of Kent to Romney, destroying it, and then on to Dover. Here he built a strong fort at the foot of East hill; from here he attacked the old Roman fort and captured it. It is said that William claimed to have won a great battle. He left a garrison there and marched along the old Roman road, Stone Street, to Canterbury. Here the people offered no resistance and they met him with 'boughs in their hands like a moving wood', so writes Kilburne in 1659. They gave him hostages and in return William allowed the men of Kent to practise their ancient privileges, remain free men and retain the 'Invicta' of the county coat of arms. It means 'unconquered and untamed'. The White Horse on a red background was the symbol of the ancient Saxon Kingdom of Kent.

With no opposition, William marched along Watling Street to Rochester and London. A well-travelled Roman road over the chalk hills was more preferable than the woods and thickets of the Weald, where he could easily have been ambushed. It was not long after reaching London that the English surrendered and on Christmas Day 1066 William was crowned King. He had conquered the English in battle and now wanted to be their legal King. It was a peaceful conquest. He stood for tradition and order and was prepared to acknowledge the customs and laws of the country. In 1067 William was forced to return to Normandy and he left his half-brother Odo, Bishop of Bayeux, as Earl of Kent. Now the men of Kent turned against him and joined William's enemy, Eustace of Boulogne and tried to storm Dover castle. When William returned, he was forced to allocate land to his Norman followers in order to keep the peace. In Kent much of the land was owned by the Church so little changed at first but by 1076 we see that the English Archbishop of Canterbury was succeeded by Lanfranc, one of William's chief advisers. Both men were great organisers and to their leadership of Church and State we owe many of the great achievements of the Norman Conquest; the comprehensive Domesday Survey of 1085, a record of land tenure, laws and population, and the fine buildings both ecclesiastical and secular in town and country remain a constant source of historical knowledge.

CHAPTER 17

A Candle Beam

SITED ON THE SHINGLE RIDGES of Dunge Ness, the 20th century
nuclear power stations dominate the landscape. From miles around
their massive hulks are faintly visible on the horizon. Nearby the
multi-coloured chalets and bungalows of the summer visitors and part-
time fishermen seem insignificant and overshadowed by the giant
concrete buildings on the foreshore. A modern road, with its bright
yellow sign-boards, guides visitors and workmen across the beaches to
this electricity generating plant. Inside everywhere is spotlessly clean.
Men in white uniforms are busy renewing the worn rods in the
underground reactor and the control room with its red and green
lights, its dials and switches, seems always alert to danger. Outside,
across the marshes to the north, the tall steel pylons carry the cables
bringing electricity to our homes, farms and factories. Today electricity
is an essential commodity, and the lonely isolated marshes and beaches
are ideal locations for its production. The 20th century has witnessed
the completion of the most modern electricity station yet devised at
Dunge Ness B. Completed in 1972, its cost was over £100 million.

What is electricity? Its essential raw materials are those which have
been used by man from very early times – water for cooling, fuel for
heating and machines to generate the energy. Man has always needed a
'power' to grind his corn, fashion his tools and weapons, spin and
weave his cloth and give him light and warmth. At first it was man
power, then wind and water, and now coal, gas, oil and electricity.

Even in the times of the Domesday Survey in Kent, machines were
driven by water power. Twenty-two mills have been recorded on the
River Len alone, and many more can be traced on other small rivers
and streams like the Loose and the East Stour. Names on Ordnance
Survey maps will quickly depict their sites. Of some, like Swallow Mill
in Little Chart, only the weather-boarded mill remains to tell its story.
At others, like Old Mill Farm at Leeds, the mill pond, the tail race and
the head race can still be seen. At Hollingbourne the huge water wheel

is intact. But Chegworth Mill on Leeds Castle Estate is perhaps the finest example. The low timber building still houses the working gear of a mill, and outside, the wheel still turns by the power of water from the River Len. Among the cobwebs and the dust, it is still easy to witness a water mill at work grinding corn for animal feed, and it is easy to imagine our ancestors dependent on a good head of water. At Swanton Mill, on the East Stour at Mersham, the white weather-boarded water mill built in the seventeenth century has been fully restored to a working mill and produces wholemeal flour. Situated on one of Ashford's new foot trails, it is open to visitors.

Wind too was a source of power. Scattered over the Kentish landscape are the smock mills and the post mills of a former age. Today some are still and silent, a reminder of the days when man waited for the wind to turn the sails and grind his corn. Too many are lost to posterity through age and decay and a lack of funds for repair. In Bethersden Mill House, Mill Road and Mill Lane are the only surviving evidence of the three working mills in the 1930's. A few, such as Mill House in Cobham, have been converted into homes, while others, like Woodchurch, have been restored and opened to visitors. The white smock mill at Willesborough, in full view from the busy M20 road, is another example. It was refurbished by Ashford Borough Council in 1991 and now, under the auspices of Willesborough Wind Mill Trust, grinds corn for bread. The barn still houses the wheelwright's shop. Yet perhaps Cranbrook has the finest sample. Renovated at great expense, it stands proud with its giant white sails erect for all to see.

By the Middle Ages, coal was an important source of power but it was not until 1912 that the first hopper of Kent coal was raised to the surface from Snowdown Colliery. Chislet, Tilmanstone and Betteshanger were open by 1928. New villages were built at Elvington and Hersden to house the influx of miners and their families. The East Kent Light Railway transported the coal to the war-time port at Richborough and in 1930 an aerial ropeway was constructed to Dover. But the problems were numerous. The seams were deep, narrow and contorted and the mines were liable to flood. However, in 1958 the Ministry of Power consented to the construction of a power station on the marshes at Richborough to use the coal from Kent's collieries. Today it is interesting to visit the Roman fort of Rutupiae on its low

Cranbrook Mill.

island hill, and look through the North Postern towards the sea. Silhouetted against the sky are three giant cooling towers belching steam beside the large modern brick power plant. Water from the River Stour and the nearby coal governed its site, but in 1972 the station was converted to oil fuel and a new port was developed at Richborough to import it.

Whether it is fuelled by water or wind, coal, oil or uranium, 'power' has always been vital to man. To many of us today a 'power cut' means no light, no heat and often no work. At a turn of a switch we cook a meal, wash the clothes, watch a TV programme, listen to a recital or work one of the computers which are a feature of every modern

Fairfield Church.

office. It is interesting to realise that only in 1942 many isolated farms, cottages and churches on Romney Marsh were still lit by candles and paraffin lamps; and yet today these same marshes provide the site for Kent's nuclear power station at Dunge Ness. And even now, almost within sight of the Ness, Fairfield Church has no electricity and in Challock Church on the Downs, a fine example of a candle-beam remains to remind us of the past.

CHAPTER 18

'Three Thousand Tons a Year of Business'

I N 1798 HASTED DESCRIBED THE River Medway at Maidstone in the following terms:

'A considerable traffic is carried on by and from hence to Rochester, Chatham and so on to London and from the several large corn mills here abundance of meal and flour is shipped off for the use of those towns, the dock and navy there . . . The fulling and paper mills in and near the town send all their manufacture hither to be transported from hence to London. The vast quantities of timber brought hither from the Weald of Kent and its neighbourhood, by land carriage as well as water, are conveyed from hence by the navigation of the Medway to the dock at Chatham . . . Besides which there are several large hoys of 50 tons burthen and upwards which sail weekly to and from London for the convenience of the town and other adjacent country.'

By Hasted's day the Medway was a busy waterway in the heart of Kent, carrying food, raw materials, manufactured goods and passengers. Maidstone was the focal point. Just below the bridge near Faith Street was the dividing line between the Upper and Lower Medway and the two companies which controlled the use of the waterway.

From very early times, craft plied upstream to Maidstone but by the early 17th century river trade was increasing rapidly. Chatham was growing fast as a dockyard town. It needed oak from the Weald for the shipyards, guns and cannon from the iron works at Horsmonden for the Navy and corn to feed the people. Likewise towns like Maidstone itself, Rochester and even London, the market for the paper from the mills along the Len and Medway, benefited from this growing river traffic. The roads were poor and unmade, dry and dusty in summer, wet and rutted in winter. Traffic was slow. The King wrote to the people of Tonbridge: 'We are given to understand that the River Medway in Kent from Maidstone to Tonbridge upwards may be made possible and useful for boats, to carry commodities . . . all the year round because the highways are bad and the bridges dangerous.'

Fish weirs were removed; the locks at East Farleigh and Teston were built and by 1630 small barges were reaching Yalding where Wealden timber was now loaded for Chatham dockyard.

The local landowners were reluctant to sell their land; the river was their private property. In 1665 an Act of Parliament was passed to make the river navigable for the carriage of 'Iron Ordinance, Balls, Timber, Wood, Corn and Grain, Hay, Hops, Wool, Leather and all other provisions there had, growing and accrueing from thence as of Coals, Limestone, Wares and all other Necessaries and Commodities Hither'.

Ten local landowners were to have a monopoly of carrying the goods. They became the Upper Medway Company. At first they were carriers, with coal as the chief commodity, using 40-ton barges to Tonbridge. Soon they were merchants, buying coal from Northumberland and Wales and selling it along the river. Perhaps the Company created the first monopoly. The merchant company expanded, buying iron from Norway as well as local chalk for lime burning and selling to the riverside towns.

For another hundred years the Upper Medway Company flourished although there were problems from coal thefts, so that 'Coal delivered by bargemen at each wharfe shall be measured as they are delivered out of the barges . . .' and from press gangs . . . 'a press gang from Maidstone had lately been up the River and taken 4 persons out of the Company's service.' Yet the Company continued to flourish and improvements were soon made in the Lower Medway at Allington and New Hythe.

In 1804 the Company advertised 'a barge carrying Shop Goods, Ironmongery and Goods in general from Maidstone to Tonbridge and places in between will load at Maidstone every Monday'. In 1828 there was a company barge travelling from Tonbridge to London advertising hops as downstream traffic and 'wheat, beans, peas, malt, oats, barley, linseeds, shop and other goods upstream'. Every village and town between Tonbridge and Rochester would have had a wharf where raw materials, food, fuel and manufactured goods would be loaded and off-loaded.

From Maidstone to London by river it was 70 miles, whereas by road it was only 36. Yet for a hundred years or so the river was a busy trading route; it was cheaper, safer and more reliable than road travel.

When the Thames–Medway Canal from Strood to Gravesend was completed in 1824, it saved about 50 miles of the journey. In 1827 Henry Drury of Maidstone advertised a weekly sailing barge service to London via the canal. He was so successful that he put on two barges and soon found he had a competitor in Henry Simonds, also of Maidstone, to sail twice weekly to London 'in 24 hours by way of the new canal'.

So passengers too were travelling along the Medway, sometimes, maybe, simply for pleasure. In 1831 a public excursion was run from Maidstone through the Canal in the steamboat *Adelaide*, offering refreshments and a band and Maidstone Commonalty Society is known to have had its annual outing up and down the Medway in a decorated barge, accompanied by a fleet of smaller pleasure boats and finishing at night with a firework display – not an uncommon sight today on festive occasions.

However, the Medway was above all a trading river. It was a vital link between the Weald of Kent and Chatham via Maidstone to London. When Henry Drury died in 1840, his Maidstone wharfmen advertised to let: '3000 tons a year of business'.

CHAPTER 19

Swift and *Sure* – A Recollection

DRIVING NORTH ALONG THE A256 towards Ramsgate, one's attention is suddenly arrested by the giant black propellors of the SRN 4 silhouetted against the steep cliffs of Pegwell Bay. It is fascinating to visit the viewing platform of the modern hoverport and watch *Swift* and *Sure* skimming the surface of the mud at low tide. Gradually the huge rubber skirt deflates and the propellors stop swinging. The hovercraft lies on the apron and immediately the foreshore is busy with people, trucks and cars. In summer thousands are sped across the Channel by Hoverlloyd for business and pleasure. Maybe the more conventional traveller in 1973 would choose 'Sealink' via the 'Golden Arrow' from London; passengers can reach Paris from Folkestone or Dover under the auspices of British Rail. Originally a Roman port, the present harbour at Dover was opened in 1909, its massive piers and breakwaters protecting it against the Channel storms. Within half a century and the advent of the motor car, it had outgrown itself, and a car-ferry terminal, recently extended, was built at the east end. Today Townsend Ferries make Dover the busiest passenger port in the world. Viewed from the cliff top in summer, there is a continuous flow of 'miniature' cars along the quayside, and it is easy to believe that 5,000,000 people passed through the customs in 1972.

In the same way as Continental passenger traffic has been revolutionised in the 20th century, so has continental trade. Even in Roman times Kent provided a link between the Continental Empire and the outlying 'provinces'; today, with London's decline, many one-time small ports are flourishing. Shipping lines save money and time by using the low-duty Kentish ports noted for the speedy unloading and 'turn-round' of vessels. Ramsgate's quay is lined with Volkswagen cars and trucks while Rochester's wharves are busy with cargoes of coal and oil, timber and woodpulp, wine and beer, canned pineapples, fresh oranges and dried onions, to name only a few. Nearby, on the banks of a small muddy creek at Rainham, modern concrete and asbestos

Hoverlloyd, Pegwell Bay.

warehouses and giant grain hoppers line the quay. The 1960's
witnessed the growth of container traffic; while Continental and
British containers, their small, inconspicuous red seals unbroken,
awaited shipment to France from Dover's Western Docks, others sped
their way to London or to Kent's inland container port, 'Freight Flow'
at Lenham.

Perhaps above all it is the road and the road vehicle which has
revolutionised Kentish transport. At the beginning of the 20th century
the country was already criss-crossed by a network of railway lines
linking the large towns to each other and to London and the coast.
Ashford, Canterbury, Tonbridge and the Medway Towns were well
served by the railway. Smaller towns and villages on these lines began
to grow because they had access to a market town, but where there
was no railway, journeys were in horse-drawn carts. These horse buses
went to the main towns once or twice a week at a speed of 4 or 5
miles per hour, a slow and arduous journey. In 1904 the first tram
succeeded the horse bus from Barming to College Road, Maidstone,
and soon the motor bus followed. By 1918 most of the larger villages
south of Maidstone had buses once or twice a week and services ran

from Maidstone to Ashford, Sevenoaks, Sittingbourne and Chatham, although infrequently. Soon dozens of would-be bus company owners were competing for bus routes until fares became ridiculously cheap and the buses raced from stop to stop to pick up passengers. Eventually the Government took control of public road transport. London Transport was established in West Kent, Maidstone & District Company in Mid-Kent, and the East Kent Company in East Kent. The bus, but above all the private car, has been all important in the transport revolution. As early as 1900 Mr Harry Smith parked his car outside his grocer's shop in New Romney; he was a motor enthusiast and set up a garage next door. A picture dated 1903 in the *Kent Messenger Centenary* has the following caption: 'A pedestrian, a cyclist, a horse and cart and one of those confounded motor contraptions!' Today these 'motor contraptions' are everywhere; they have caused a social as well as a transport revolution. More cars mean more leisure and a demand for more leisure pursuits. More cars means a need for more and better roads between towns, to London and the coast for speedier and safer travel. The Thanet Way (1930), the Maidstone by-pass (1960) the M2 (1963) were built for speed; built so that heavy goods vehicles and through traffic could avoid the narrow streets of old towns like Rochester, Sittingbourne and Faversham. In West Kent, Sevenoaks and Tonbridge are by-passed and in 1972 a new stretch of motorway from Aylesford to Wrotham has improved the A20 Dover-to-London road. Even now our roads are congested; in our towns parking meters, traffic wardens, pedestrian crossings, one way streets and multi-storey car parks attempt to overcome the problems of an ever increasing volume of traffic. In the countryside petrol stations, flyovers, laybys, clearways and motels are all evidence of the importance of road travel in the 20th century.

But Kent's nearness to the Continent has always been a challenge. In North Falls meadow behind Dover Castle an outline of the monoplane marks Blériot's landing place after the first Channel flight in 1909. Perhaps Kent played its greatest part in air travel during World War II when it was so vulnerable to German attacks. Scattered over the Kentish landscape are the remnants of war-time air bases, such as Great Chart, where huge signs, 'Beware flight path,' often hindered the progress of local traffic. Others, such as Biggin Hill and Manston, remain in civilian guise while Dan Air Skyways Ltd at Ashford Airport advertise frequent services to Le Touquet and Le Bourget. Throughout the centuries Kent has always looked towards the Continent. Today all major roads and railways lead from London to the coast and so to France by 'Skyway', 'Sealink', or 'Hoverlloyd' and perhaps in the next decade via the 'Chunnel'.

Today, at the beginning of the 21st century, the 'Chunnel' is no longer a dream but a reality.

CHAPTER 20

The Shipwrights

B ATTLESHIPS AND FRIGATES, tea clippers and mail steamers, wherries and hoys, lifeboats, smacks, yachts and submarines; all these vessels have been launched from Kent's shipyards since 1488 when *Great Harry*, the 'first ship of the Royal Navy' was built at Chatham. During these centuries ships have changed; they have been built of wood and iron, steel and fibreglass; they have been propelled by sails, steam, oil and nuclear energy; they have been used for defence, for trade and for pleasure.

Kent had numerous advantages for the shipbuilders. It had a long coast line with small creeks, natural harbours and long, winding estuaries. Faversham grew up in such a creek. In 1588 its shipyard built, manned and equipped a 40-ton vessel, *Hazard*, to fight against the Spanish Armada. By 1900 James Pollock and Sons Ltd. had established Kent's largest commercial shipyard, building paddle steamers for sale to Brazil and a paddle ferry, the first to cross the Atlantic under its own power. In the 1920's Pollock was one of the first to install oil engines in small coasters; but the creek was small and development was limited. The firm specialised in designing and building small cargo ships, tugs and barges. In 1970 the yard closed, yet only recently the local newspaper reported that a vessel had been launched from the creekside at Faversham. It was a 155 ft. floating restaurant called *Father Thames* built by Southern Shipbuilders (London) Ltd. The Company employed 60 local people and the 'sounds of clashing steel and humming presses' were heard once again on the creek. Faversham was busy again; the yard had orders for a luxury motor launch in aluminium alloy, two trawlers for Peterhead and a yacht for a South American sport-fisherman.

There were many small harbours around our long coastline which from the Middle Ages had been important for defence and trade. Faversham was one of these, and so was Tenterden, now 12 miles from the sea. Its coat-of-arms depicts a ship with sails spread; perhaps

63

Tenterden is derived from 'Inter Den', 'the slipway of the Dens' (of the Forest of Anderida). Tenterden men built ships at Small Hythe (the small harbour); next time you visit Ellen Terry's Museum, look for the square pond in the garden which is a part of the basin where Henry VIII came to see one of his ships being constructed.

Right from the beginning the Medway had really been the hub of the shipyards. Its width and winding course gave plenty of space and its marshy banks could easily be reclaimed for cheap development. Two of the Royal dockyards, Chatham and Sheerness, were there; and since the launching of the *Great Harry*, kings began to see the need for ships, particularly for defence. Henry VIII saw powerful enemies on the continent; Queen Elizabeth, in spite of her desire for peace, saw potential enemies in France and Spain. Although *The Sun*, a warship, had been built at Matthew Baker's yard in Chatham in 1586, it was not until Cromwell's time that the Medway's shipyards grew to importance. By Napoleon's day war and trade encouraged the growth of the shipyards. Frindsbury, Rochester, Upnor and Gillingham, as well as Sheerness and Chatham, had eleven private yards besides the two naval dockyards. Names like Brindley and Hawker are well-known.

Trade increased the demand for ships and shipbuilding the growth of trade. Cargo ships had been built for individual merchants, who needed vessels to trade abroad and along the Medway, particularly in goods which supplied the Naval dockyards and the shipyards. At first English timber was used: oak, ash, elm and beech from the High Weald were brought along the lower Medway. These were supplemented by the import of Baltic fir for masts and yards. Tar, tallow and turpentine came initially from the Baltic, then from the new colonies across the Atlantic. Iron for the fittings and for ammunition came first from the ironworkings of the High Weald, Lamberhurst and Horsmonden, but by 1720 from Germany and Russia. Hemp for the ropes was grown in England and the sails were made from English and Scottish flax. In 1839 the *Alecto*, the first fighting steamship in the Royal Navy, was built at Chatham. The demand for new and better raw materials grew and the size of the vessels increased until the Medway shipyards were too small. The Medway's importance declined; Tyneside, Teesside, Merseyside and Clydeside grew. The numbers of shipwrights, riggers, caulkers, sailmakers, engine-fitters and boiler-makers decreased. Yet in Chatham today it is fascinating to see from the river the modern submarine-building yard and the gleaming funnel of the latest nuclear submarine side by side with the long three-storey red-brick building of the ropery, where all the Royal Navy's ropes are made.

Ships are still being built and repaired in Kent today. As well as Faversham creek and Chatham dockyard, there is Ramsgate Marine Ltd. in Ramsgate Harbour. There are shipwrights, marine engineers and chandlers working in mahogany, plywood, pine and fibreglass to repair all types of small craft. When I visited them in March there was a trawler, a pleasure-boat and a P.L.A. vessel on the slipways. I was particularly interested to hear that this firm is responsible for the maintenance of all Trinity House pilot vessels. So Kent still plays a vital role in the nation's shipping.

CHAPTER 21

To Police Kent

DIAL 999. The sirens wail, blue lights flash and the police cars speed to the scene of a bank raid, a rail crash, a hotel fire or a motorway pile-up. The Kent Operations Room at the Police Headquarters in Sutton Road, Maidstone is the centre of activity; telephone number 999. Whatever the place, whatever the crime, vehicles are speedily despatched to the emergency. A radio network, telephones, teleprinters and new computer technology distribute messages hither and thither throughout Kent, Great Britain and abroad.

It was the 14th January, 1857 when the Kent County Constabulary, a force of 222 men, was formed; its task: 'to police Kent'. The only qualification 'for a hefty and healthy looking young man' to join the force was the ability to read and write. The first Chief Constable, Captain John Henry Ruxton, founded his force on 'fair play and no nonsense', and the first order he issued instructed his recruits what was expected of them: 'Carefully to consider and recollect that alone, by the continual exertion of each member of the force and his zealous, active co-operation with the Chief Constable . . . in maintaining the discipline . . . of the service, can the great aim and object of the County Constabulary be attained, viz: the prevention of crime and the maintenance of good order.' Within three months labourers, soldiers, sailors, clerks and mechanics had formed an efficient team of police officers in the original headquarters at Wren's Cross, Stone Street.

Even as early as Roman times there were officers to enforce laws. Their duties were numerous; their tax collectors were infamous. And throughout the Middle Ages there were 'tithing men, reeves, sheriffs, watchmen and parish constables'. The power of the village constable was limited to his own parish and parishioners rarely ventured beyond the parish boundary. He was responsible for mustering the King's soldiers, maintaining arms, collecting taxes, rounding up the non-church-goers and protecting common lands from would-be pros-pectors. Dependent on the whims of the local squire, administration and penalties varied from parish to parish. Right up to the 19th century, the village constable was still responsible for law and order, but after the formation of the Kent County Constabulary in 1857, he came under the control of the central authority at Wren's Cross.

One acre at this old site accommodated the administrative offices, criminal investigation, barracks and training school, tailor's shop and stores, stables, a parade ground and paddock for the horses. In those days communication was a problem. There were no telephones, a poor telegraph service (morse code), roads were cart tracks and the railway era had only just begun. The Chief Constable had a horse and trap and in 1890 12 dog carts were bought for the superintendents and the first mounted police force was established. 1896 saw the introduction of police bicycles and 1911 the motor cycle. In 1923 'Lizzies', the police Ford cars, were first seen in Kent.

In the 'prevention of crime and the maintenance of good order' the new Police Constabulary had its problems. It was the time when long stretches of railway line were being constructed throughout Kent. Travel was a privilege for the wealthy, but at the same time it became easier for intending criminals to evade the law. They would travel too, and prize fights were commonplace, set up anywhere along any part of the track which was unguarded by the police. Problems also arose on the roads. There were no radar scanners, and the speed limit in town and village was 2 m.p.h. Vehicles exceeded the speed limit. It is said that if a policeman had to walk briskly to pass a steam roller, its speed must have been greater than 2 m.p.h. There were problems too in detecting a criminal. There were no finger prints, only footprints. When the owner of the boots was located and the individual nail markings checked, he would be charged. One interesting anecdote is recorded. A constable was asked in court whether he could swear that the prisoner was at the scene of the crime. 'All I can swear, Sir,' he replied, 'is that if he was not at the scene of the crime, his boots were.'

Today, it is a far cry from the days when the constable's uniform was an embroidered blue frock coat at four guineas a piece, but his task is still the same, 'to police Kent' – 'the prevention of crime and the maintenance of good order'. Crime and disorder have increased but the modern police force, with specialist branches, is well equipped. Traffic patrol crews, regional crime squads, the river police, the mounted police, frogmen and the C.I.D., to name but a few – all these are household names to us whether in fact or fiction. Just dial 999.

CHAPTER 22

The *Invicta*

ON MAY 3RD, 1830 Kent's first railway line was opened, linking Canterbury to Whitstable. From contemporary paintings it is easy to visualise the scene that day. Small clusters of people gathered on the steep banks overlooking the single track. They cheered and waved as the steam engine *Invicta* pulled the open wagons towards Canterbury. It was a day to remember. Within a span of 100 years a network of railways criss-crossed the Kentish landscape – single track and double track, passenger and industrial, main line and branch. They linked town to town and village to village, but above all, they linked Kent to London and London, via Dover, to the Continent.

The Canterbury-Whitstable line was the first passenger route, providing the speediest and easiest journey between Canterbury and Whitstable and then, by a daily packet service, to London. By 1842 the South-Eastern Company had built a main line from Redhill (Surrey) to Ashford via Tonbridge, Paddock Wood and Headcorn. Its prime function was to carry local traffic. Within two years it had been extended eastwards to Folkestone and Dover, and so to France or Belgium in one day. Family holidays at the seaside resorts grew, first Folkestone, then Dover, then Thanet, when in 1846 a line ran from Ashford to Canterbury, Ramsgate, Broadstairs and Margate, and then on by a branch line to Sandwich and Deal. In 1927 the narrow-gauge line from Hythe to Dymchurch and New Romney was opened and a year later extended to Dungeness. The journey is 14 miles along the coast of Romney Marsh. This, too, increased the holiday traffic. Today it has become a valid commercial venture with ten miniature coaches drawn by steam engines. Dr Syn of Russell Thorndyke fame has been the delight of many small boys. Last year the first priority of my Japanese visitors, in Kent for one day only, was to travel on a small steam train.

So with the railway era passenger traffic was booming. Holiday resorts, villages and market towns like Canterbury and Ashford flourished. Industry, too, grew with the railway lines. By 1849 the Weald and much of Kent had been opened up and the South-Eastern Railway Works was established at Ashford. Lines linked Strood with Gravesend, Swanscombe, Greenhithe, Stone and Dartford to London and within ten years Maidstone was linked to the Medway towns via Snodland.

It is interesting to notice the early development of industries in these areas, such as the Holborough Cement Works in Snodland. Industrial companies also built narrow-gauge lines to carry their raw materials and employees. The Sittingbourne and Kemsley light railway was built in 1906 by Lloyd Ltd (now Bowater Scott) and a light railway carried wagon-loads of pulp and china clay from the company dock at Ridham on the Swale to the mills at Kemsley and Sittingbourne. Closed to industry in 1968, two miles of line were preserved for the tourist, or more, perhaps, for the railway enthusiast. On its special Open Day, the line carried 500 passengers through the industrial landscape. The newspaper report described it as 'through the ugliest, most despoiled and acrid-smelling waste in the land.'

With the growth of the railways and industrial development, the distribution and density of population changed. From the 1870's the greatest development was in north and north-west Kent: through Beckenham, Bromley, Chislehurst, Sidcup, Bexley, Erith, Crayford and Dartford a network of railway lines grew. One third of Kent's population lived here. As the population grew, so did industry and north-west Kent became an integral part of Greater London.

It is fascinating to look at a map of this one hundred years of railway building. The Kentish landscape played a large part in the pattern that was created. On the whole, the natural advantages of the landscape were utilised. The Vale of Kent allowed the building of the straightest line in Kent, between Redhill and Ashford, but the giant viaduct, with its 19 arches in Folkestone today, is evidence of the engineering skills of the 19th century. The Vale of Holmesdale linked Ashford with Maidstone; the natural river gaps through the North Downs, carved by the Medway (Maidstone to Rochester), Stour (Ashford to Canterbury) and the Darent (Sevenoaks to Swanley) and the coastlines of the Thames River, the Estuary and the Channel shore were all assets for the railway engineers of the 19th century.

The railways built and owned by private companies competed for

trade in goods and passengers. By the end of the 19th century the
South-East and the East Kent Companies (later London, Chatham to
Dover) had amalgamated into the South-Eastern and Chatham
Railway Company. Only recently a friend of mine bought a railway
chair engraved 'S.E. & C.R.' – perhaps a commemorative piece, but
certainly a telling record of Kent's private railway era.

By the end of the 20th century our railways had been nationalised
and de-nationalised by subsequent governments, and the
unremunerative lines had been axed by Dr Beecham. The world's
smallest railway, from Hythe to Dungeness, was recently saved from
closure by McAlpine Ltd. You have only to pass the station at
Rolvenden on the original Kent and East Sussex Railway to see the
brightly polished engines and wagons waiting to carry the weekend
tourists to Bodiam Castle. Today's railway enthusiasts work hard and
lovingly to preserve Kent's railway history under the auspices of the
Railway Preservation Society. As we move on into the 21st century,
passenger travel and trade are expanding into Continental Europe.
Eurostar and the Channel rail link constitute the greatest feat of Kent's
railway history. The new rail line now being built across Kent will be
one of the achievements of the new Millennium and the upheaval in
Ashford and along the route has to be measured against the benefits of
faster travel and its inevitable rewards. At the same time, the excavations
are adding knowledge to the existing records of the past and our
history is being preserved for future generations to enjoy. Only last
week the newspaper recorded that a 17th-century timber-framed barn
at Charing Heath on the line of the Tunnel Rail Link has been
dismantled and is being re-built section by section in Tenterden, using
the traditional skills of earlier craftsmanship.

Yet perhaps it is Canterbury that owns the greatest souvenir of
Kent's railway-building era. For Robert Stevenson's *Invicta*, built at
Newcastle upon Tyne for £625 and used on the 1830 Whitstable-
Canterbury line, was bought by Sir David Salmons in 1906 and
presented to Canterbury. It is in the Dane John Gardens for the
historian and visitor to enjoy.

CHAPTER 23

'Sweete, Newe and Good'

T**HE TINY HISTORIC CHURCH**, a row of old cottages and the 'local'
are lower Halstow today. It is quiet and isolated on the banks of a
muddy creek. Its salt flats and marshes provide a habitat for the sea-
loving asters and pinks, and a haunt for hundreds of wild geese.
Standing on the sea 'wall' and looking towards the Medway it is easy to
understand why the Halstow Creek was an important oyster ground in
the 17th century. It belonged to Sir Robert Darell of the Manor of
Barksore. In 1634 he leased it to John Pett for a rent of £10 and
records tell us that 'six bushells of the best oysters being sweete, newe
and good and four barrells of sweete, newe, good and well conditioned
pickled oysters' were delivered half-yearly.

Kent's oyster beds from Strood to Whitstable were the best in
England. It is quite possible that even as early as Roman times oysters
were important in Rochester. In any case, Whitstable 'natives' were well
known by the Romans, who exported them. By Medieval times strict
regulations were put on oyster fisheries. Beds were protected from
over-exploitation. In Faversham the Company of Free Dredgers paid
rent to Henry II for their oyster beds. We know that in 1630 400
people, a quarter of Faversham's population, were dependent on oyster
'dredging' for their livelihood.

Defoe remarked in his *Tour of Great Britain, 1724* that 'oyster fishing
and ale houses were the principal occupations of the people of
Queenborough.' Rochester's fisheries were controlled by the
Rochester Oyster Fishery. Strict rules were imposed on members. No
oysters were dredged before sunrise, after sunset, or during frosty
weather. The time of year, the size of a 'stint' and the number of 'stints'
per day were likewise controlled. Marketing was regulated very strictly.
The greatest markets were local towns and London. Boats were
ordered to berth by the town quay in order of arrival from the beds.
We know that in 1688 Maidstone had a wharf for landing and selling
oysters and other fish. By the 17th and 18th centuries Flemish boats

came up the Swale and the Medway and loaded up with oysters to supply a foreign market.

Right from the Middle Ages onwards, fishermen were vital to the life of the country. Not only oysters but 'floating fish' were also very important. Dried or salted herrings provided the greatest bulk and demand increased with the growing importance of the Church and the insistence on fast-days. It was inevitable that the Kent coastal towns became the chief source of supply, being so near to London. One of the duties of the Cinque Ports, according to their charters, was 'to catch the nation's fish'. Rye (Sussex) was obliged in Tudor and Stuart times 'to furnish the Royal household daily with fresh fish.' Autumn was the season for the great herring catch and the small fishing boats would be seen moving north from the Kentish ports for Medieval Yarmouth (Norfolk), then a small island in the mouth of the Yare where nets were dried and mended and the fish cured. The island and town belonged to the Cinque Ports with charters giving them rights of 'den and strand' (dunes and shore) right up to the 17th century.

It is interesting to notice today that only Dover and Hastings (Sussex) of the original Cinque Ports retain their fishing interests. However, many fascinating hours can be spent around the harbour at Folkestone (a Cinque Port 'Limb' of Dover), watching the daily comings and goings of the fishing fleet and listening to the antics in the nearby fish market at The Stade, or talking to the weather-beaten old 'salts' who linger on the quay, having spent a large part of a lifetime on the deck of a local trawler. At low tide the drifters and trawlers sit on the mud in the small harbour but as the tide flows, they begin to bob up and down and soon preparations are being made for sea.

It is a familiar sight to see the vessels nose their bows around the harbour arm while a small crowd gathers for the auction. Daily some three or four tons of fish are bought and sold on the auction slabs: cod, skate, plaice, herrings, sole. There are still more than a hundred fishermen in Folkestone today. Generations of their families have worked before them to haul out as many fish as possible in the five 12-hour journeys they make each week and to sell them 'sweete, newe and goode' off the marble slabs at The Stade.

Folkestone Harbour.

CHAPTER 24

The *Monthly Mirror*, September 1805

KENT WAS AGAIN OPEN to attack from an invading army. It is said that Napoleon had boasted, 'with three days' east wind I could repeat the exploit of William The Conqueror.' He was massing his forces at Boulogne and seemed likely to cross the Channel. New defences had to be built, existing fortifications reinforced, and above all a volunteer army was needed. This was the Napoleonic scare.

The *Monthly Mirror*, in September 1805, read 'The Martello Towers are at length begun to be adopted by the Government in the neighbourhood of Folkestone. Four of them are in a great forwardness within a quarter of a mile of the town just at the bottom of the hill, where they command the beach and cross each other at right angles so as to produce great havoc on an invading army.' Today these round brick towers stand on a green sward, a continual reminder of our vulnerable shoreline. In all, 74 of them were built along the coastline of the marshes. Each one cost £10,000 and needed 7,000 bricks, which were brought in barges and landed on the beaches. Each one was 30ft high and equipped with a 24-pounder gun mounted on a platform; the ground floor contained a powder magazine with a reservoir and stores of food and ammunition for 22 men. By now many have been destroyed; some have been converted into houses; and one at Dymchurch is repaired and open to the summer visitors.

Our beaches were further protected by improvements on existing fortifications. The medieval castle at Dover was transformed into an entrenched camp for 5,000-6,000 men. Earth ramparts were constructed behind the walls. The ditches were deepened and the medieval underground passages cut into the chalk were made stronger with additional guard rooms. The graffiti on the walls of the keep are evidence of its use as a prison for French soldiers.

To stop the invaders from moving inland, the Royal Military Canal was built as a second line of defence. It follows the foot of the old cliff line from Hythe to Rye, 27 miles long and only 60 ft wide. Every

A Martello Tower, Hythe.

quarter mile there was a break in the line of the canal, and at each bend an embrasure was constructed for heavy cannon. Completed in 1806, its real need was over in 1805, when Nelson defeated the French and Spanish at the Battle of Trafalgar. It cost about £140,000 to build and was never a military success; yet it had, and still has, an economic value. Heavy goods were carried along it from Rye to Bonnington, where a field is still called 'Coal Wharf'. Taxes were levied on the barges and canal station houses were built for the tax collectors; one can be seen at Appledore Bridge. Today the canal plays an important part in keeping the marshes habitable and farmed because water from the criss-cross ditches flows, or is pumped, into the canal and so to the sea to drain the Dowels, 650 acres of land just below sea level.

The threat of a Napoleonic invasion saw the introduction of a military camp at Shorncliffe, one of our most important camps today. In 1796 the earliest 'telegraph' system was set up to send messages from the coast to London. A line of hill-top semaphore stations 6-8 miles apart relayed coded messages in just two minutes from Deal to Shooters Hill (London).

Above all men were needed. Volunteers came from the Cinque Ports

The Royal Military Canal, Appledore.

and their limbs, and all able-bodied men between 15 and 60 years from every Kentish parish. Out of Folkestone's 3,200 population in 1798, the records show there were 215 who were already soldiers, sailors or privateers and only 140 volunteers – 9 horsemen and the rest foot soldiers. They guarded our shore defences and fought at the Battle of Trafalgar, in which the French fleet was destroyed and Nelson was killed. His body was brought ashore at Sheerness dockyard for its journey to St. Paul's Cathedral. But Nelson's great victory was not Napoleon's defeat. The final campaign was the Battle of Waterloo in 1814 where the French were defeated by the Duke of Wellington and his men. A model of part of the battlefield of Waterloo, made by Captain Siborne, a surveyor in 1838, can be seen in Dover Castle.

Every year many holiday-makers in Ramsgate will have strolled along Military Road or The Plains of Waterloo or admired the fine Regency Terrace in Wellington Crescent without a thought for the Kentish men who embarked from Ramsgate harbour to defend our shores against a French attack.

CHAPTER 25

The Viking Ship

ON THE COAST OF PEGWELL BAY is the model of a Viking longboat ship. Today, frequently repainted for the benefit of the tourist, it is gay and resplendent in its historic setting. King Alfred of Wessex, of which Kent became a part in 825 A.D., was determined to fight off the threats of the Danes and the Norsemen (Vikings) who were harassing his countrymen. These new invaders were pirates who had plundered and burnt towns and villages on the Continent and were now attacking and raiding Kent. They were tough; they wanted money and land; or perhaps some were just adventurers and Kent was particularly vulnerable.

They sailed up the Thames and over to the Isle of Sheppey. Their ships were very efficient when skilfully handled. About 78 ft long, they were built of overlapping oak planks. They had one square sail, 16 oars on each side, and one oar near the stern steered the vessel. They were brightly coloured and decorative and equipped with a tilt which could be erected for shelter at night. Such a vessel has been excavated on the coast of Norway. King Alfred built his navy by levying a tax – eight hides, a helmet and a coat of mail for one vessel. His ships, according to the Anglo-Saxon Chroniclers, 'were long ships. Some had 60 oars and others more, shapen neither like the Frisian nor the Danish, but so it seemed, to him they would be more efficient'.

The English met the Danes in 850 A.D. off the coast of Pegwell Bay. It was the first naval battle ever fought by an English fleet and it was disastrous; Alfred's ships proved very inefficient against the skill of the Viking sailors.

The Danes continued to ravage and plunder. They wanted wealth and this was to be found in the monasteries, Canterbury, Rochester, Reculver, Lympne, Minister-in-Thanet and Minster, Sheppey. During a visit to the peaceful village of Minster (Thanet) and its Abbey today, it is often difficult to imagine these dark-haired pirates plundering the Minster and burning the Abbess and her nuns; but the story tells how

The Viking Ship, Pegwell Bay.

the body of the first Patroness, St. Mildred, was untouched and was taken in safety to Canterbury.

King Alfred had failed at sea; he had to succeed on land. The English were farmers living in small family groups, the earliest form of village communities. They were farmers and now King Alfred had to wield them into his army. They were armed with spears and shields and were opposed by the mounted infantry of the Vikings, who were armed with steel caps and ring mail. In 892 they invaded with 250 ships, bringing their horses with them and sailing up the Rother to Appledore. Here they built an encampment, destroying a nearby fort and palisade of King Alfred's. The next year they returned, sailing up the Swale with 80 ships, and landed on the marshes near Milton Regis, building a fort, probably that nowadays known as Castle Rough. King Alfred stationed his army about halfway between Appledore and Milton Regis. However, the Danes continued to raid the surrounding villages and apparently met with little resistance and little in the way of counter-attack. Before long Alfred made peace with the Danish leader, Heasten, who withdrew his men across the Thames to Essex. The raids were over; the Danes had left little mark on the 'Kentings' or English villages. There are no Danish settlements and Kentish place names show no evidence of Danish influence. Yet the Viking ship remains on the cliffs above the Bay as a reminder of these North European pirates.

In 1971 the newspaper reported that a ship, thought to be of Viking style from about 900 A.D., had been found by the driver of a Kent River Authority bulldozer whilst working on the North Kent Marshes at Graveney. Built of oak and abandoned beside a waterway, it was carefully dismantled and taken to the Mary Rose Trust in Plymouth to be conserved before being displayed in the National Maritime Museum, Greenwich.*

---

*Today, September, 2000, it is still undergoing conservation. Archaeological knowledge and techniques have advanced in the past 30 years and the Graveney vessel is now believed to be an Anglo-Saxon trading vessel dated circa 1000 A.D.

CHAPTER 26

The Kentings

EVEN BEFORE THE ROMANS were forced to leave Britain in 400 A.D. to defend Italy, new invaders were coming across the North Sea. The forts at Richborough, Reculver and Stutfall were built as a defence against these intruders. Fifty years later these foreigners were beginning to settle in small communities along the valleys of the Stour, the Medway and the Darent and along the East coast from Margate to Dover. They were the 'Kentings', or simply the people who lived in Kent. In 730 A.D. Bede, in his *Ecclesiastical History of England*, referred to them as 'the Jutes'. From later archaeological discoveries we have found out much about them: their homelands, their way of life and their customs. By studying their jewellery, excavated from burial grounds, and comparing it with finds on the continent, we know that the Jutes came from the German Rhineland and from Frisia (N. Holland). Records tell us that in the sixth century brooches of iron or silver with mounted garnets were made at Faversham and also in the Rhineland. The Jutes were craftsmen working in precious metals, gold and silver, but also in bronze and iron.

Although we know that the Romans knew about Christianity and practised it in Canterbury (St. Martin's) and Lullingstone, the majority of the Britons and the incoming Jutes were heathen. Most Jutish finds have been collected from single burials or cemeteries, but judging from the 'finds', they did believe in an after life. Perhaps the most interesting discovery was at Lenham in 1946. A Victorian wall was being removed from a 15th Century Hall House when three skeletons, with a sword, spearhead, two daggers, bronze buckle and three shield studs were discovered. They were believed to be part of a 6th-century cemetery. The house is now a chemist's shop called The Saxon Pharmacy.

It was during this period of history that Christianity was brought to Kent by St. Augustine and his monks. The earliest Kentings settled in family groups. They came in small bands, with a leader. Kent was already a Kingdom ruled by a King. In 449 King Vortigern, unable to defend his Kingdom, called on two Jutish leaders, Hengist and Horsa, for help and in return promised them the Isle of Thanet. They landed at Ebbsfleet, under the banner of a rampant white horse, the origin of the white horse of the county Coat of Arms. The story goes that Horsa was killed in battle and Hengist betrayed his trust, turned against Vortigern and became King. Whether this is true or false, it is certain that at this time Kent was a Kingdom ruled by a king. King Ethelbert (560-616) was probably the most famous, since he accepted St. Augustine and his Christian beliefs. From this time Christianity gradually became established in Kent, and was centred in Canterbury and Rochester. The kings of Kent used their power and began to make laws. The same practice can be traced in the Rhineland too. The Church was to be exempt from taxation and heathen worship was forbidden.

During the Jutish period the first communities began to grow, the families or clans settled in groups and the place became the home or 'ham' of the head of the family. Examples are the Godmaers – ham (Godmersham) or the ingas or ing (people) of the chief – Dyttel-ingas or Dyttel's people (Detling). Other places were named after local features, a bridge, a ford; others still became Woodchurch, Broomfield, Oldbury.

From finding their cemeteries, their weapons, their jewellery and by studying their place names we can find out where the Jutes lived. Right up to the eighth century they settled in the valleys and along the coast. By then the population of Kent was increasing, probably to about 50,000. New lands had to be found and the resulting later settlement was in the Low Weald on the thickly wooded, heavy clay lands. Place names reflect this: 'den', a woodland swine pasture, e.g. Bethersden or Beaduric's swine pasture; and 'hurst', a knoll or wooded knoll, e.g. Lamberhurst or Goudhurst. These villages consisted of small huts grouped around a hall, the chief's house, with a moat, a well or spring, and the whole being surrounded by a ditch and bank and a wooden palisaded fence. Such were the origins of the English village of today. 'Ham', 'Hurst', 'Ingas', 'Den', 'Hythe' (a landing place) 'Leigh' (a glade) 'Smeeth' (a Smithy) are Anglo-Saxon or old English words. The 'Kentings' were English.

CHAPTER 27

St. Martin's, Canterbury

S<small>T</small>. M<small>ARTIN</small>'<small>S</small> <small>IN</small> C<small>ANTERBURY</small>, with its inconspicuous medieval tower, its Kentish flint walls, its thin Roman bricks in the Chancel and its stone font, is the only church in Britain where Christians have worshipped continuously for 13 centuries, or even longer. Some suggest that the Romans worshipped there. Certainly we know that the Romans were Christians; at Lullingstone in the Roman villa we can still see the remains of painted wall plaster depicting figures of saints with their arms extending on either side in the early attitude of prayer.

When St. Augustine came to Kent in 597 A.D., there were few Christians, although the records tell us Bertha, King Ethelbert's Queen, worshipped in the first small 'stone-and-brick' church on the site of St. Martin's.

St. Augustine was a Benedictine monk sent to Kent by Pope Gregory, with 40 missionaries, to bring Christianity to a 'pagan' country. Imagine him, in his long monastic robes, a huge silver cross and a large painted and gilded picture of Christ borne in front of him, as he set foot on the Kentish shore. He landed at Ebbsfleet on the Isle of Thanet and immediately sent word to the King. Ethelbert agreed to see Augustine in a field by the sea, where today there is a stone cross to commemorate this meeting. Although Ethelbert was superstitious, he listened and promised the monks a home in Canterbury, his capital. From Ebbsfleet the monks crossed to Richborough and then by the Roman road to Canterbury. Perhaps we can imagine them holding their banners and their silver cross and chanting hallelujahs.

At first they worshipped in the chapel at St. Martin's, Queen Bertha's church; soon King Ethelbert and his court accepted Christianity and were baptised, possibly in the stone font still seen in the Church today. St. Augustine was ordained Archbishop of Canterbury and founded a monastery to the east of the city, the Abbey of St. Peter and St. Paul. In 605 A.D. Augustine died and was buried in the north porch of the Abbey Church. Today in ruins, the Abbey is a peaceful place in which to reflect on the teachings of these Benedictine monks.

The missionaries who landed with St. Augustine at Ebbsfleet in 597 A.D. played their part in spreading Christianity. A second English diocese was founded at Rochester.

In 669 A.D. Theodore of Tarsus, a Greek scholar, was appointed by the Pope as Archbishop. He and his scholarly monks built up the library in Canterbury, attracting more scholars to the city and founding King's School.

In the countryside throughout Kent a simple wooden cross marked the place for worship in many villages. Then small churches of wood or stone gradually grew up, directed by a priest from one of the new smaller monasteries, Lyminge, Reculver, Minster-in-Thanet or Minster-in-Sheppey. Although no one Saxon Church remains, evidence of the work of these Christians can be seen incorporated in later buildings such as St. Martin's and in the stonework of the north aisle in Lydd Parish Church.

CHAPTER 28

The Gunfounders

IN HORSMONDEN, the village inn used to be called 'The Gun'*. In
the early seventeenth century John Browne, gunfounder, was
employing 200 men in his ironworks nearby to make guns and cast-
iron cannon balls for James I. Ammunition was in great demand and
John Browne had a flourishing foundry. Ever since Roman times the
Weald of Kent had been a source of wealth; the reddish-brown and
ochre-coloured ironstone nodules found in the local sandstone were
smelted here. The Wealden forests, of oak and beech, were cut and
burnt by the charcoal burners, providing the fuel for the smelters.
Many streams, dammed back into vast ponds, could give enough water
force to work a wheel. Heavy equipment was needed: huge hammers
for beating or forging the iron; and huge bellows for kindling the
charcoal, as well as kilns, 38 feet high, for smelting the ironstone.

The wheels, driven by water pounded back in the large ponds, drove
the bellows which fanned the charcoal at the bottom of the kiln.
Continually fed in at the top were shovelfuls of ironstone and charcoal.
The iron melted out of the rock and was drawn off into shallow
troughs; it was brittle and impure. So it was reheated and beaten with
giant hammers, again driven by the water wheel. The smoke and smell
from the furnace and the continual thudding of the hammering made
the industry too dirty and noisy to be carried on at home, so suitable
sites were found outside the villages and many local names remind us
of this. Near Biddenden there is a house called Hammer Mill, a stream,
Hammer Stream, and there was a pond (now dry) which covered 30
acres, the Hammer Pond.

The need for fuel, ironstone, water power, kilns and machinery
made this industry an expensive one. This meant that usually the
wealthy gentlemen of the locality, such as the Bakers of Sissinghurst
Castle, the Darells of Scotney Castle, or the Filmers of East Sutton,

---

*Recently it has been re-named 'The Gun and Roast Spit'.

would finance the venture and then let it to another family to work it. So in 1614 John Saunders leased Gloucester Furnace, Lamberhurst, from Sir Edward Filmer. His rent was based on the amount of iron he produced there and in 1672 it is recorded that he was paying £24 per annum.

Although guns were one of the main products of the Wealden iron industry, once the iron had been forged by the huge hammers, it was fit for the local blacksmith to make horse shoes, nails and hinges, household utensils, firebacks and rivets. Hasted, in his *History of Kent* even tells us that the people of Lamberhurst claimed that the railings in the Whispering Gallery in St. Paul's Cathedral were cast at Gloucester Furnace.

However, by the end of the seventeenth century, with the discovery of better iron ores in Northern England, and of the value of using coke for smelting, the Kentish iron industry was collapsing. The Wealden villages were soon peaceful again. Today only the fine ironwork of the firebacks, the stray cannon-balls found buried on new building sites, and the names of inns, fields and streams, are evidence of this once flourishing industry.

CHAPTER 29

Shipway

ON 2ND JUNE, 1953 the Mayor of Tenterden, in full regalia, joined
the procession of dignitaries from Westminster Hall to the Abbey
at the Coronation of Her Majesty Queen Elizabeth II. He had been
chosen from among the Mayors of 'the Ports' to represent them on this
historic occasion. Four of 'the Ports' or the Cinque Ports are in Kent:
Sandwich, Dover, Hythe and Romney. In return for providing ships for
the King, the burgesses or barons of these towns were given certain
privileges. One privilege is retained to this day – the 'Honours at
Court'. A Baron of a Cinque Port (a mayor today) was given the right
to bear the canopy over the King or Queen at the Coronation to
imply 'the Ports'' responsibility for the safety of the island from sea
attacks. In 1953 the Baron carried a banner. A section of the canopy, in
cloth of gold, carried at the coronation of George III can be seen in
the Guildhall, Sandwich.

The Cinque Ports, Sandwich, Dover, Hythe and Romney in Kent
(and Hastings*) in Sussex) were all in vitally strategic positions along
the coast facing out across the narrowest part of the Channel and so
most vulnerable to attack from foreign raiders. They were important
ports in sheltered channels or bays or at the mouths of rivers. They
were essential to Edward the Confessor, who needed ships to repulse
the Danish raids or to ferry him and his men and goods across to
France. Each town had to provide 20 ships, each with a crew of 21
men, for 15 days per annum, in return for certain privileges. These
ships were small cargo ships, passenger ships, warships and fishing
vessels all in one. Several illustrations of them can be seen on the
famous Bayeux Tapestry. The Arms of the Borough of Hythe shows a
similar ship, with high stern and forecastle, one mast and yard, and with
a large square sail. Take away the castellated erection at bow and stern,
and it becomes a fishing boat.

---

*Rye was a Limb of Hastings. Tenterden had become a 'Limb' of Rye (Sussex) in 1499, and therefore a
member of the 'Confederation of the Cinque Ports'.

SHIPWAY   87

The 'Ports' became very powerful. Kings needed ships and granted charters to confirm the Portmen's privileges. In addition to the privilege of 'Honours at Court', the Ports were exempt from tax but were still allowed to levy them and to claim all 'flotsam and jetsam brought ashore by the sea or wrecks'. Hythe still possesses the historic document recording the grant made in 1298.

Perhaps the chief privilege was 'Den and Strood'. The Portmen were not just sailors; they were traders and above all, fishermen. 'Den and Strood' gave them the right to land fish at Great Yarmouth and to dry their nets, sell their fish and take control of the herring fair. This was highly important to the fishermen because the Kentish ports were far away from the fishing grounds and their greatest difficulty was to sell the fish.

Against the Portmen the King was helpless. About 1150 a Confederation of Cinque Ports had been established, with a Court of Shepway (Shipway). Its task was to supervise the duties, and particularly the privileges, of the Portmen. The chief officer was the Lord Warden of the Cinque Ports. This office was combined with that of Constable of Dover Castle. It meant that he was a Royal Officer appointed by the King, but he took an oath to uphold the privileges of the Cinque Ports. Today this office is held by Queen Elizabeth, the Queen Mother. The Court of Shipway still exists and meets occasionally, but has no power.

During this time many smaller ports had become Limbs (or members) of the Cinque Ports. Examples are the port of Ramsgate, a Limb of Sandwich, and Folkestone, a Limb of Dover. They helped the head Port to provide vessels and men and in return shared in the privileges. They, too, had their Court, less formal than the Court of Shipway, and known as the Court of Guestling (a village near Rye).

By 1400 the importance of the Cinque Ports had virtually ended. After the Great Storm of 1284, when the Rother changed its course and reached the sea at Rye, ships could no longer sail into Romney Harbour at the foot of the church tower. Should you visit New Romney today, hunt for the 'tethering hook' (as the locals tell) still found in the churchyard perimeter wall and seen on the front cover of this book holding a small anchor and rope, which seems most appropriate. The sea also built up a shingle bar at Hythe so that the old town is a mile from the shore and the original Dover Harbour was

The West Doorway, New Romney Church.

silted up and is today the site of the town, with its streets, shops and houses. Only Sandwich remained and by 1500 the Wantsum Channel and Sandwich Harbour too began to silt.

The original Cinque Port documents make fascinating reading. The last full ship service was in 1444, when the ports contributed '5 ships of 60 tons burthen, with a crew of 58'. One ship had an armament of '2 pieces of brass, 2 fowlers, 12 calivers and 15 muskets. For sustenance there were 2,000 biscuits, 30 mail of beef, 100 salt fish, 2 cwt. bacon, 1 cwt. butter, 1 cwt. of cheese and 14 tuns of beer.'

Only five small ships were sent by Kent to fight the Spanish Armada in 1588. 'The *Elizabeth* of Dover, 120 tons, *Reuben* of Sandwich 110 tons, *John* of Romney, 60 tons, *Grace of God*, Hythe, 50 tons, *Hazard* of Faversham, 38 tons.'

With the silting of the Channel ports, the Cinque Ports went into decline, but the Portmen were not to be deterred. The Cinque Ports might have lost their lawful means of livelihood, but the Court of Shipway had lost its power over them. The wars of the seventeenth century were financed by means of heavy duties on tea, spirits, tobacco, snuff and silk. The Cinque Ports justified their free trade as a privilege. The Portmen of Ramsgate hauled their kegs of brandy at midnight up the steep wooden steps of Jacob's Ladder at the same time as the Romney Marshmen were defying the 'Preventive Men' and 'trading' their fleeces for untaxed 'brandy and baccy, laces, and a letter for a spy', as Kipling has written.

CHAPTER 30

'New Town' or 'Railway Family'

IN 1846 185 ACRES OF LAND were bought by the South Eastern Railway Company for £21,000, for Ashford had been chosen as the site for a 'Locomotive Establishment'. Already the town was becoming the focus of railway travel. The main line to Redhill via Tonbridge (1842) to Ashford and on to Folkestone (1843) and Dover (1844) and the main line from Margate via Canterbury to Ashford were completed, with more to follow. Ashford was a town in the midst of agricultural countryside with no other established industry. The 185 acres on the south side of the Folkestone line were soon developed, where 'not long since were fields seldom trodden except by the foot of the herdsman'. The locals will agree.

Right from the beginning, the 'Railway Family' grew in South Ashford. The Company built 'New Town' and the design proved to be the forerunner of Council schemes some 80 years later. It was a complete village to house employees so that by 1912 there were 272 houses built in ribbon fashion of a traditional industrial type. The whole was centred round a spacious green. The huge building housing the Ashford Works Mechanics' Institute and the Public Baths stood prominently between the Alfred Arms and the 'New Town' village shops. Finally there was a school and a church, Christ Church, South Ashford. This 'railway' church was consecrated in 1899, paid for by the voluntary subscriptions from shareholders of the South Eastern Railway Company with its upkeep maintained by railwaymen until 1937. By the early 20th century the great expansion of the works was making greater demands on the railway company. More housing was needed, another school and further opportunities for education. It was not long before the Mechanics' Institute provided classes in 'machine drawing and construction, railway carriage building, French, shorthand, arithmetic and geometry'. The 'Railway Family' at 'New Town' grew and flourished with the 'Locomotive Establishment'. Visit the 'village' today and you will still recognise many of its original features; its green, its pubs and its Institute, but its rows of terraced houses, six-roomed dwellings of 1912, are fast disappearing. Street names remain. Cudworth Road, once a long, drab row of industrial housing, is historically significant.

James L'Anson Cudworth was a locomotive designer and became the first manager of the Ashford works. He was responsible for the selection of equipment for the new works and an extract from an article in George Meason's *Official Guide to the S.E. Railways* in 1861 makes it possible to achieve some insight into the immensity of the task.

'These (locomotive and carriage) works consist of the large engine shed, 280 feet long by 64 feet wide . . . the engine repairing shops and a large crane capable of lifting 20 tons . . . machine shop or turnery . . . tender shop . . . smiths' shop . . . wheel hooping or boiler shop . . . carriage and truck house capable of holding 50 carriages and 80 trucks . . . store room . . . a perfect model of neatness . . . machines – unwieldy and huge in bulk to the most diminutive screw, the whole arranged with greatest precision and elegance.'

Cudworth and his followers were responsible for new designs in railway locomotives. In 1861 he designed the first Mailing-class locomotive for hauling the Dover Post Office Express from Cannon St. to Ashford in 75 minutes. It was known as 'Flyers' and was the fastest in England.

James Stirling equipped the engines with steam reversing gear and improved the carriage designs so that by 1888 it was reported that the third class carriages on the Ramsgate to Hastings line 'are more roomy than the average in England'. Within 10 years Harry Wainwright had designed the Folkestone car train, provided with armchair first class accommodation.

The Wainwright era was a period of great progress at the Works. With the amalgamation of the London, Chatham and Dover Company and the South Eastern Company came automation. An automatic fire-extinguishing plant and a coke crusher, a power house and electrified overhead cranes were installed in the Ashford Works, the only ones in any works in the country. Early in the 20th c. a chemical laboratory and an electro-plating plant were added and in the 1940's parts for the railway's first two mainline electric locomotives were built. Two world wars saw changes in output. In 1914 and in 1939 the Works played its part in the war effort, producing armour plating for bomb trolleys and ramp wagons for tanks.

Ever since the inauguration of the Works, the community involved has been essentially a 'railway family' in a railway 'New Town'. Even the employees can be traced from father to son through generations. It is recorded that in one family alone twenty-one descendants of the first coppersmith have been employed at the Works through the decades. Today the 'Locomotive Establishment' is still in Ashford and many redundancies have been prevented by its work for the export market. In the seventies, at a time when the 'status quo' was still in evidence, a contract was entered into with Yugoslavia.

During the last three decades the Railway Family has changed beyond recognition. The Works are redundant, the buildings converted for light industry and Ashford now offers a two-hour rail journey to Paris via Eurostar. The 'family' has faded but the 'soul' remains. Since the pioneering days of 1846 the British Rail system has changed dramatically and Ashford prepares itself for the new Millennium.

CHAPTER 31

'Chiefe of Ye Quakers'

WHEREVER WE MAY TRAVEL in town or village in Kent, our attention is inevitably drawn to the church. Whether it is the tiny Norman structure at Barfreystone, with its intricate stone carvings, or the massive pseudo-perpendicular tower at Burham, the church dominates the village. On the other hand, it may be Benenden by the green or Goudhurst on the hill, or the quaint, squat Fairfield, standing alone on a low, artificial mound on Walland Marsh; in any case, the church is the prominent feature of the landscape and right up to the seventeenth century it was the focus of every community. Religion was a vital part of life. By law only one church, at first the Catholic Church and later, in Tudor times, the Church of England, was recognised by the State. But by 1640 dissension had begun to spread.

Perhaps Kent was particularly vulnerable to new ideas. In many parishes there were scattered communities of farmers and foresters, a long way from the church and often cut off from the village in winter by impassable roads. These conditions gave many Kentish people a tradition of independence of thought and attitude, making them an easy prey for Dissenters. Again, there were the 'refugees' from the Continent, the Walloons and the Dutch families living in Canterbury, Sandwich and Maidstone and practising their crafts. Because of their language and customs, they were always regarded as 'foreigners', and they soon formed their own Churches under 'foreign' parsons. In fact, non-conformity in Kent was so rife that in 1635 Archbishop Laud reported to Charles I that 'there are many refractory persons to the government of the Church of England about Maidstone and Ashford and in some other parts.' Yet dissent continued to flourish; the Justices were unable or unwilling to enforce the laws of the Church.

Apart from the immigrants, most of the Non-Conformists were tradesmen and craftsmen. Consequently they were very active in the Wealden area, in the clothing districts through which the clothiers travelled to London. They came into contact with foreign merchants who bought their cloth and the clothiers in turn talked to the weavers, spinners and carders when they delivered and collected materials. These people were easy converts because their livelihood depended on the clothier. There was George Hammond, a tailor of Cranbrook, who 'taught' at Frittenden, Biddenden, Benenden, Bethersden and at Lenham. Here the Vicar noted that 'one Hammond, who lives six or seven miles off, comes there sometimes preaching and endeavours to draw aside the weaker people as women etc.' It is recorded too that a meeting held in 1671 at the home of 'one' Susan Garret in Cranbrook consisted of '6 board weavers, a clothier, mason, butcher, brazier, 2 shoemakers, a tallow chandler, 2 gardeners, 2 simple women and a widow, all from Cranbrook and Hawkhurst'.

In 1672 32 parishes, some Baptist, others Congregational, applied for licences for Presbyterian Ministers and Meeting Houses in East Kent, the Weald and in the towns of West Kent. Visits from George Fox, the son of a Leicestershire weaver, began a Group of 'Friends', and by 1668 monthly meetings were being held in Canterbury, Cranbrook, Folkestone and Rochester. It is recorded that in Dover 'Luke Howard, a shoemaker, is "Chiefe of ye Quakers"'.

So today, as well as the Church in towns and villages, scattered throughout Kent, there are the chapels of these Dissenters. Look for the tiny, inconspicuous, weather-boarded Baptist Meeting House in Cranbrook, almost hidden by the homes of its one-time congregation, or the large, plain edifice of Bound's Cross, Biddenden.

CHAPTER 32

Great Harry

G*REAT HARRY* was the first ship of the Royal Navy. It was built in 1488 at Chatham, then a small farming and fishing community. The villagers lived only a stone's throw away from the muddy creek which was to become the Royal Dockyard. These local men became the smiths who forged the nails and chains and the sawyers sawing planks for the clinkers and decking. Then there were the rope-makers, twisting the yarns for cables and rigging, the carpenters and joiners, caulkers, sail-makers and mast-makers, pitch-heaters and shipwrights. Soon these local inhabitants were joined by skilled craftsmen from the Deptford and Woolwich dockyards. By 1512 the first dock was constructed where the *Great Harry* had been built. The chalk cut from the hill slope was thrown along the muddy foreshore to raise it above high water. This was the beginning of Chatham dockyard. By Queen Elizabeth's reign, Sir John Hawkins had charge of the dockyard. It is recorded that he 'sent to sea' ships 'in such condition, hull, rigging, spars and running ropes, that they had no match in the world either in speed, safety or endurance.'

The Medway provided an ideal site for a Naval station guarding the approaches to London. The waterway was tidal and sheltered from the south-westerly prevailing winds by the chalk hills, Along the banks there was space on the mudflats for grounding ships for repair. By 1547 the Naval Dockyard had been established and Upnor Castle was built to protect the ships and stores. Soon the river was defended by an iron chain which could be stretched across from the castle to Chatham to prevent enemy ships from reaching the dockyard. It is recorded that in 1635 the repair of the hulls of 7 ships cost £6,000. By 1665 800 men were employed in the yard to build the dockyard's storehouses and yards and to build and repair ships.

Supplies were needed. The Weald of Kent was the chief source of the oak and elm for dockyard buildings. It was brought by land to the Medway at Yalding and then sent to Chatham by water. Bricks and tiles were made in Kent for the storehouses and dockyard walls. Local smithies forged the anchors, locks and chains. By the end of the century the ironware was coming from Sunderland (Durham). Chatham looked out towards the Continent and it was easy to import hemp from the Baltic and canvas for sails from France, but guns came from the gunsmiths at Horsmonden. Small items such as lanterns and candles were made locally in the Dockyard Town. Now Chatham was vulnerable in wartime. The Dutch, under Admiral de Ruyter, sailed up the Medway in 1667 and fired at Upnor Castle. Defences were inadequate. Even the iron chain failed to stop the Dutch plunderers. Warships on the river bank were set on fire and destroyed. Samuel Pepys records in his diary that the Commissioner was 'in a fearful stink for fear of the Dutch'.

A century later the most famous ship constructed at Chatham was launched. She was Nelson's *Victory*. Nelson spent his childhood in the streets of Chatham and learned his skills of seamanship along the Medway. William Pitt has described his visit to Chatham for the *Victory* launching.

'In the dockyard everything was hustle and bustle. Men were seen knocking out the great wooden supports and finally greasing the slipway with huge slabs of Russian tallow and mutton fat. The dockyard and stands were packed with excited sightseers as the *Victory* gracefully slid down the slipway.' In 1805 Nelson met the French and Spanish fleets off Cape Trafalgar.

Re-organisation and improvements had continued since the building of the *Great Harry* and Chatham had become a Naval Station as well as a ship-building and repair yard and a garrison town. It had changed from using wood to iron in the building of ships. As Charles Dickens tells us, 'It resounded with the noise of hammers beating upon iron and the great sheds and slips under which the mighty men-of-war are built loomed business-like . . . Great chimneys smoking with a quiet, almost lazy air, like giants smoking tobacco . . .'

It changed, too, from sail, steam and oil to nuclear power, from *Great Harry* and the *Victory* to frigates, destroyers and nuclear submarines. But inns like the 'Jolly Caulkers', 'The Shipwrights' Arms' and the 'Ropemakers' Arms' still conjure up pictures for us of its historic past.

CHAPTER 33

The 'Bat and Ball'

'G'D MORNING, SIR', said the elderly gent as he ordered his pint. 'You'll be busy today – there's cricket on the green,' and the conversation continued as other locals joined in to share their memories. I looked out over the green sward which would host yet another game that afternoon if the weather held fine. In many Kentish villages the green is still the local cricket ground – Woodchurch, Bourne, Boughton Lees, Bearsted and Matfield are but a few. Meopham had the added attraction of the 'Cricketers' Arms', where spectators and players can enjoy a gossip and a pint after a friendly match. On the other hand, 'St Lawrence' Canterbury, 'The Vine' Sevenoaks and 'The Mote' Maidstone, all quickly remind us that cricket is a county game. They conjure pictures of 'the week' in mid-August, of thousands of spectators in the pavilion stands, of the prominent AA and RAC markers signposting the route and of the traffic congestion, but above all of the quiet concentration of the cricket crowd. On such a day it is hard to believe that the pavilion, annexe and restaurant at St. Lawrence were not built until the beginning of the twentieth century, and that once everyone used to adjourn to the 'Bat and Ball' for bread and cheese and a pint of ale.

It is difficult, too, to believe that records at Newenden give the date of the first game of cricket there in the 1300's and it was another 300 years before it became popular and began to attract spectators. By 1675 it is said that every cottage in the cricket-playing districts in Kent had 'a well-greased bat either kept on the bacon rack or hung up behind the kitchen door.'

A century later 20,000 spectators were recorded at Bourne Park. Perhaps the popularity of cricket at that time is best understood by Mr Bunby's 'The Cricketers'. He wrote: 'Then of cricket, of cricket we'll cheerfully sing, for a game of such innocence pleasure must bring.'

Yet cricket hasn't always been an acceptable sport to be enjoyed. In 1629 a curate in Ruckinge was brought before the Archdeacon's Court because 'he many Sundays last summer, after he had read Divine Service, in the afternoon did immediately go and play at Cricketts in very unseemly manner with boys and other very mean and base persons in our parish.' Thirty years later six Cranbrook men were indicted at Maidstone Assizes for playing 'the unlawful game of Cricketts'. To the Puritans the playing of any game on a Sunday was a serious offence but 'Cricketts' was to grow in popularity and become a County game.

Dartford provided the setting for the first county cricket match in 1709, between Kent and Surrey. Edwin Stead of Harrietsham became the first Kent cricket patron and by 1744 scores and players' names were published. They were the local tradesmen, perhaps gardeners, carpenters and bootmakers.

Canterbury was the headquarters of Kent cricket. The St. Lawrence ground was bought in 1896 although the 'Gentlemen of Kent' had played in the first cricket week in 1842. The scores recorded:

'1st Innings: Kent 278, England 266
2nd Innings: Kent out for 44, England won by 9 wickets.'

New names began to attract spectators. Alfred Mynn was an 'attacking batsman, a fast bowler, renowned for his good looks and recognised by his close-fitting jersey bound with red ribbon'. So the records say. Today he is remembered for the Mynn Memorial Institute which honours deserving Kent cricketers. Among the great ones of the twentieth century were Colin Cowdrey, Alan Knott, Derek Underwood and Mike Denness but above all, the name of Lord Harris must be recorded in the history of Kent cricket. He was a Kent patron, Captain in the first Test Match in 1880, and played against Australia in 1884. By securing the St. Lawrence Ground for Canterbury, he saved the future of Canterbury Week. An afternoon spent at Belmont, the family home, is always a delight. A stroll through an avenue of walnut trees leads to the iron gateway, his cricket pavilion and now disused pitch. He is remembered in Canterbury and in Throwley Church.

In January, 1999 a headline in *The Guardian* read: 'Ancient Tree's Long Innings Coming to an End'. It told the story of the 185-year-old Lime on the boundary of the St. Lawrence Ground. It is even incorporated into the club rules. 'If a ball touches any part of the tree, it is deemed to be four runs.' A young tree has been planted nearby which will be lifted into the hole left by its ancestor.

CHAPTER 34

The Gateway to London

K ENT HAS ALWAYS BEEN VULNERABLE. Throughout the centuries it has been the 'gateway' between London and the Continent – the 'gateway' to traders, travellers and invaders. The Romans and the Saxons invaded the Kentish shores and settled here. Then King William came this way in 1066. As he approached, he would have been sighted from the fortified town or borough on the cliff top at Dover. The Saxons had built a church, St. Mary in Castro (some Saxon work remains) beside the Roman pharos, incorporating it into their township; but there was no castle. After his victory at Hastings, William marched to Dover. The Norman chronicler, William de Poitiers, tells us that he spent eight days adding fortifications to the Saxon borough. In fact he built the first castle at Dover. It was the first Norman castle in Britain, but nothing remains of it today for the visitor to see. It would have been a ditch and bank and a wooden palisade within the Saxon borough.

The Normans were a conquering race. They needed to build their castles quickly to show their power and intimidate unfriendly townspeople. There was plenty of local timber and plentiful unskilled labour. The Saxon Chronicle records that in 1067 William went over to Normandy and his regents, Bishop Odo of Bayeux and Earl William remaining in England 'wrought castles widely throughout the realm and oppressed the poor folk, and ever thereafter greatly grew the evil.' Their early castles were uniform in character. A lofty conical mound of earth was surrounded by a deep ditch. At Dover the site was naturally defended on the steep chalk spur, but at Tonbridge an artificial mound 40-50 feet high was built. Historical research and excavations have revealed crescent-shaped enclosures surrounded by ditches and banks; these were the baileys. On these banks were lines of wooden palisades and the central mound was encircled by wooden stockades and 'crowned with a wooden tower on its top'. This was the Norman mount or 'motte'-and-bailey castle. The timber was vulnerable to attack and fire. In the twelfth century the Normans began to use stone.

In the 1180's Henry II undertook the building of Dover Castle in stone, costing £7,000. It is fascinating to study the stone used in the construction of the great tower keep with its 20-feet thick walls, the towers, gates and walls of the inner bailey and the curtain wall of this strong Norman fortress. Look for the courses of Roman tiles, the flint nodules, knapped flints and huge blocks of Kentish ragstone, Caen stone from Normandy and limestone from Dorset. Seen from the air, its defensive site is clearly recognised, a township or fortified borough or a 'little city'. Even as long ago as 1597 one visitor is said to have written 'upon a hill, or rather rock which on its right side is almost everywhere a precipice, a very attractive castle rises to a surprising height, in size like a little city extremely well fortified and thick set with towers and seems to threaten the sea beneath.' Today it is still a fortress and houses a garrison

The Normans built their castles for defence. Kent linked London to the Continent and the main lines of communication were by sea, by road and by rivers. So castles were built at strategic points along these routes. Dover guarded the Channel and was at the southern end of the Roman road from London via Rochester and Canterbury. At Rochester, Watling Street crossed the River Medway. The Romans had realised its importance and the medieval castle and cathedral were built within the wall of the Roman city. Today a seventy-feet square keep stands dominant on its hill, looking out towards the river crossing it once defended. Norman arches with chevron mouldings remain and the whole original 'castrum' site is surrounded by remnants (well preserved) of the Roman and medieval walls. Canterbury, too, guarded the crossing of a river, the Stour, on the great road running from London to the coast. Completed in 1174, its castle stands on an earth bank outside the city wall, close to the river. Its eleven-feet thick walls of rough flint and rubble masonry with Caen stone quoins is typically Norman.

It might be said, too, that the Normans built their castles to defend their townships. Dover, Rochester and Canterbury were important medieval towns as well as being strategically sited on route ways. Tonbridge castle on its artificial motte, with its great fortified gateway, is yet another example of a township and river crossing which had to

Leeds Castle.

be defended. Maidstone had no castle although sited on the tidal
Medway. The Romans had avoided the valley but a castle was built at
Thurnham on Watling Street to guard the north–south route. Built on
a chalk spur, it commanded a wide view southwards. The road had to
be kept open for travellers, free from marauders and hostile local
barons. Today there is only a small section of the bailey wall remaining;
the rest has been plundered as a local building material.

Medieval kings even as early as King William were often prone to
reward their followers by granting land. These noblemen built fortified
homes against attack. Cooling Castle on the edge of the Thames
marshes was one of these 'castles'. It was fortified by Lord Cobham
after the French raids in 1379. Today the moat, walls and gatehouse
remain in a delightful setting of gardens and woodland. A plaque on
the wall of the gatehouse reminds us that Lord Cobham built this
castle as 'a natural defence, not for his own aggrandisement'. Allington
castle too, a fortified house built in the late thirteenth century, and
restored at the beginning of the twentieth, is today a delight to visitors.
Yet perhaps Leeds Castle near Maidstone is the perfect example in
Kent of a Norman castle and a fortified manor house on one site.

Robert de Crevecoeur built a castle on a small island in a lake. Through the centuries it has been added to until in the late eighteenth century Mr Wykeham Martin re-built and restored the castle as we see it today. It is only half medieval and its park is entirely the creation of the eighteenth century landscape gardener, 'Capability' Brown. Lord Conway has described it well and captures its atmosphere today. 'Motorists . . . may catch a glimpse through an opening in a pine wood of the loveliest castle in the whole world. It rises, shapely, majestic and serene from two islands in the middle of a lake. Its battlemented front and the later house behind are both reflected in the calm waters, themselves set like a pale jewel in the green and golden slopes of a lovely park.' Now, at the beginning of the twenty-first century, it provides 'accommodation' for conferences and seminars and a beautiful setting for annual musical events in the 'park'.

Whether it is the massive keep of Dover, the towered gatehouses at Tonbridge and Cooling, the curtain wall at Rochester, the steep chalk spur at Thurnham or the moat and battlemented walls in the midst of the delightful parkland landscape of Leeds, all are constant reminders of the fact that in Medieval times Kent was the foreigners' 'gateway to London' and the home of the Norman invaders.

CHAPTER 35

The Kentish Yeoman

RIGHT UP TO 1425 the ancient system of land tenure of Gavelkind persisted in Kent. When a man died, his land was equally divided between his sons. These were the Kentish yeomen of the Middle Ages. Gavelkind increased the number of small estates and so the number of yeomen. Fields in East Kent in the Middle Ages were large and unenclosed, but were often held in strips. The open fields, perhaps, owe their origin to the chalky soils, where hedges are slow-growing, but Gavelkind accounted for the strip fields. If three fields were inherited by three sons, each one of them inherited strips in each field, so that good land and poor were shared equally.

In the Middle Ages the land was not owned by the Kentish Yeomen but just 'held' by them. The whole of Kent was divided into large estates. These were manors or demesnes owned by the king or by the Church, but seldom by laymen. The 'lords' employed a bailiff in each manor. These tenants-in-chief held the land in return for payments, usually in kind, off the land, but occasionally in money. The 'tenants-in-chief' employed tenants to work for them, again receiving payment in kind. Gradually, with the system of Gavelkind, the large estates held by the tenants-in-chief dwindled in size and the number of people holding land increased.

The Church was the greatest landowner in the Middle Ages. Christchurch Priory owned 21 manors. It is recorded that Monkton Manor had '34 staff and 17 ploughmen, 4 shepherds, 2 cowherds, 1 swineherd, 1 harrower, 3 stackers, 3 drovers, 1 lambherd, 1 sower, 1 cheesemaker'. Demesne or Manorial farming was prosperous. One record shows that 'pasture was ploughed and manured, the clay was dressed with chalk, cattle and sheep provided wool, milk, meat and manure and peas and beans were grown to feed them' By the standards of the twenty-first century, agriculture was both intensive and organic. In the open fields the tenants used their strips for wintering their animals, with temporary fencing but they also had the right of common grazing on waste land.

The Archbishop of Canterbury held 25 manors. Part of the medieval farmhouse on the Manorial farm at Charing still survives today. At the beginning of the thirteenth century farming was prosperous. A century later the wool sales had decreased and corn production declined. There were severe storms and the sea flooded the low-lying land, followed by a drought which killed large numbers of sheep and cattle. In 1348 the Black Death, a plague brought in from the Continent, wiped out whole villages. People died and their houses were destroyed to prevent the spread of this 'pestilence', which 'left barely a third part of mankind alive', as one Canterbury monk recorded. At Dode only the church remains and at Paddlesworth, near Snodland, only a barn, once the village church. This meant that the number of labourers was reduced. England was at war with France and the French were making forays into towns and villages along the coast and pillaging them. To pay for the war, the Government imposed a poll tax based on wealth. Farms became places of discontent. The tenants were dissatisfied with their manorial lords and the tax collectors, finding it difficult to collect the taxes, became unpleasant and violent. In 1381 the tenants rebelled and under their leader, Wat Tyler, the 'peasants' revolted, fighting for their right to be freemen. Tyler led them to Maidstone and then on to Canterbury and Wye where they seized and burned the manorial records of land ownership and tenure and the records of labour services and rents. They met the King, Richard II, on Blackheath (then a part of Kent, though long since absorbed into London), who made promises to the rebels. They returned home but within a year rioting broke out afresh, with more destruction of property and loss of life. Canterbury, Wye, Cranbrook and Biddenden were a few of the centres of the rioting but in spite of Wat Tyler and the Peasants' Revolt for freedom, the Law of Gavelkind and the Manorial system lingered on. The Kentish yeomen gradually increased in numbers and also in wealth and power.

From 1750-1850 was the period of 'enclosures'. In Kent this meant fencing in parts of rough common and waste land or marshland for cultivation by the wealthy yeomen. Bromley Common, now in Greater London, and Barming Heath were partially enclosed in this way but William Cobbett recorded in 1822 that some commons, as at Bromley, soon reverted to their original use because the soil had proved so infertile. So, in spite of enclosures, Commons still remain as a relic of the old Feudal system of land tenure in Kent and are jealously guarded by Preservation Societies. Hothfield Common, owned by the Ashford Borough Council and managed by the Kent Trust for Nature Conservation is conserved for posterity. In the past the villagers had the right to graze animals and cut peat on the Common. Today a Nature Trail has been laid out for the enjoyment and instruction of visitors. Tiny remnants of common land survive as 'greens' in many of Kent's villages today, such as Horsmonden, Woodchurch and Benenden.

CHAPTER 36

'Who'd Ha' Thought It?'

There are old pubs and new pubs, big pubs and cramped pubs, village and town pubs, but above all there are historic pubs. The 'William Harvey' in Willesborough is a picturesque old pub opened in 1963. A strange remark until one realises that in 1963 the building was already 400 years old. Dr William Harvey lived there in 1600 and the brewers have converted his cottage into a 'new old pub'. You will probably know of other 'new old pubs' in your locality. Certainly wherever you live, by the sea, by a river or creek, on the Weald, on the Downs, in town or country, your 'local' will be interesting historically.

Ever since ale has been brewed in Kent there have been ale houses brewing their own ale. Ale was once a necessity of life; 'ale for breakfast, ale at midday or ale for supper'! There were the small ale houses for farm labourers and drovers like those in Chaucer's Canterbury Tales, 'who were entertained by a homely ale-wife'. As early as the sixteenth century, Henry VIII tried to put some restriction on the selling of ale. Shakespeare, in his *Measure for Measure*, reminds us that ale houses were kept by barbers and shopkeepers. The first owner of 'The Three Horseshoes' at Lower Hardre in about 1666 was probably the local blacksmith.

Ever since there have been travellers there have been inns and innkeepers. Originally the early inns only provided accommodation for travellers. Many of these were associated with the Church and catered for pilgrims. In the Middle Ages rich and poor would ask for a night's lodging in a monastery. Parishioners from outlying districts were expected to attend church each Sunday and on the Church festivals. These people might find shelter in church porches or in the 'parvise' over the porch. One of these can still be seen at Woodchurch. By the fourteenth century, the vicarage, once a place of hospitality, became less so and inns were built on Glebeland. Around the countryside today the many pubs called the 'Bull', derived from *bulla* or seal, can often trace their origins to the Church. The 'Bull' at

Sittingbourne was first licensed by the monks at Chilham Castle in the twelfth century. Throughout Kent the sign is in evidence in Dartford, Malling, Otford and Rochester. In Dickens's day the 'Bull' at Rochester could be relied upon, as Mr Jingle said: 'A good house, nice beds and recommended boiled fowl and mushrooms.' When Dickens gave a reading of some of his works at 'Fountains Inn', Canterbury in 1861, he wrote: 'An excellent house tonight and an audience positively perfect . . . *Copperfield* wound up in a real burst of feeling and delight.'

By 1672 six stage coaches were running from London to Kent and when public authorities began to improve and maintain the roads, yet another type of inn was needed – the coaching inn. Its heyday was in the reign of George IV but perhaps it is timely to remember that the Romans were the first great road builders and road travellers. The earliest of all signs for wayside inns is the 'Chequers', a sign found throughout England on the sites of Roman roads. It was an indication of a money changer. The chess board was an early ready reckoner. An example is 'The Chequers Inn' in High Halden, just off the line of a Roman road. Is its origin, in fact, much earlier than we think? There are others at Doddington, Laddingford and Aylesford, and in Tonbridge, where it still retains its cobbled courtyard. Apart from these, a number of coaching inns can still be recognised in Kent. It is easy to imagine what a busy coaching inn the 'George' at Aylesford must have been, situated as it is at the corner of High Street and Bridge Street. It would have been a hive of activity with its stables and yards full of horses and ostlers and its coffee room crowded with guests. The 'Royal Star' in Maidstone is an eighteenth-century coaching inn. The low arch into the yard remains today. At the 'Five Bells' at Ringwold near Deal the rings in the wall of the public bar still survive from the days when horses were hitched to them.

More exciting, perhaps, are the smugglers' inns, isolated and never too far from the sea. The 'Ship Inn' at Dymchurch is one of these. Its long, low front facing the sea and its low-beamed ceilings and secret cupboards and stairways in the walls have all been made famous by Russell Thorndyke in the Dr Syn novels. Here it is easy to conjure up the picture of dark lanterns and oil lamps, flowered waistcoats and three-cornered hats. Then there are the 'Woolpack' inns. At Warehorne there is still the flap in the church door where smugglers 'posted' their

'The Chequers' Inn, High Halden.

wares. Until quite recently a Tenterden publican could have shown any visitor a pipe in the floor of the snug leading to barrels in the cellar.

Some inns are just named after famous or infamous men like the 'Sir Thomas Wyatt' and 'The Duke of Wellington', while other names like 'The Yew Tree', 'The Windmill' and 'The Ship on Shore' have an obvious derivation. Whatever their origin, some pubs in Kent are 'locals' in the true sense: friendly places where villagers meet to gossip over a pint

By 1751 the shooting lodge at Mystole House had become the 'Penny-Pott Ale House' 'for the keepers, woodmen and teamsters grubbing trees'. Maybe the ale was subsidised to a penny a pint. Is it true to say, then, that the sign outside the Kentish pub usually reflects its historical associations? If this is so, what, then, is the origin of 'The Cardinal's Error' in Tonbridge, 'The Spy Glass and Kettle' at Wigmore and the 'Who'd Ha' Thought It?' at Rochester?

CHAPTER 37

1538

THROUGHOUT MEDIEVAL TIMES the Church played an important part in the life of the community. The monasteries, such as St. Augustine's Abbey and Christ Church Canterbury and St. Andrew's Rochester, were great landowners. By the year 1300 there were thirty such houses in Kent, owning enormous estates throughout the county. The farming families, tenants-in-chief, tenants and yeomen were dependent on them for their livelihood. Apart from this, the Church held a vital role in the social life of the community. Early in the thirteenth century the Black Friars (Dominicans) and the Grey Friars (Franciscans) founded houses in Kent, for example in Canterbury. They went out preaching and teaching and won the esteem and affection of the people by their poverty, kindness and simplicity. Hospitals too were religious houses. They provided help for the sick and the old and gave hospitality to poor travellers, particularly pilgrims. Many such houses can be traced along the main routes between Dover or London and Canterbury. Examples are St. Bartholomew's Hospital, Sandwich and the Maison Dieu at Ospringe. The pilgrimage too was an important part of medieval life. Many would journey to the shrine of a saint to give thanks or to ask help, leaving money and jewels as offerings. Perhaps the most famous shrine in all England was that of St. Thomas Becket in Canterbury and thousands made pilgrimage to it. At the end of the fourteenth century Chaucer wrote his *Canterbury Tales*, giving impetus to the Pilgrimages of his day. Not only in Canterbury but elsewhere throughout the county, St. Thomas was commemorated by Chaucer's contemporaries. In the 1970's a painting of the scene of his murder was uncovered in Brookland Church and only the other day I was delighted to see a bas-relief of the saint at Godmersham. But St. Thomas was not alone in attracting pilgrimages. Records were always kept of the 'offerings' made, which often greatly increased the wealth of that church. All too often among the less scrupulous, this led to dishonesty, as history records at Boxley. Here the monks installed a

St. Thomas (bas-relief) Godmersham Church.

crucifix which bowed and smiled at the generous gift and scowled at the meagre one. But all this was to change.

Henry VIII quarrelled with the Pope, was excommunicated and declared himself Head of Church and State. In 1538 he addressed a summons to 'Thomas Becket, one time Archbishop of Canterbury, charging him with treason and rebellion'. His Reformation was the final blow to an already declining Church. Many religious houses had never recovered from the scourge of the Black Death. By the 1520's St. Augustine's had only 31 monks compared with an original 150, and the Cathedral Priory at Rochester had only 20 instead of the former 60. At Higham in 1521 there were only three nuns. So a number of monasteries and nunneries were in fact closed before the 'inspectors' travelled from house to house in 1535 to 'look for faults'. Hospitals and small houses were immediately 'dissolved' and by 1540 the larger ones came under Henry's axe, fell into disrepair and eventual ruin. Pilgrimages ceased and the shrines were demolished, buried or burnt.

In Kent the results of the Dissolution of the Monasteries were threefold. The number of poor 'travellers' and vagabonds increased. Monks and nuns now joined the beggars, although a nominal pension of £4 per annum for monks and £2 for nuns was granted. Priors and abbots received greater compensation according to the importance and size of their house. The Prior of Christ Church was granted £80 per annum and the Prioress of Malling £40. The Church estates were redistributed. By Act of Parliament all monastic possessions reverted to the Crown. Some were kept by the King, some were immediately granted out again to Cathedral Dean and Chapter, as happened at Christ Church. Others were sold or granted to a courtier. Sir Thomas Cheyney, Treasurer of the King's Household, was given Davington Priory and Faversham Abbey and Sir Thomas Wyatt acquired Boxley Abbey, Aylesford Priory and the manors of East and West Farleigh.

Above all, however, in our county today, many reminders still survive of the dereliction which resulted from Henry's Reformation, although some religious houses, once in ruins, have been restored and re-occupied. Amongst the great restorations we must number West Malling Abbey, Minster-on-Thanet and Aylesford Priory, almost entirely re-built on its original site by the Medway. Less well known, and set high on the Downs near Dover, are the remains of another important medieval monastery, St. Radegund's on the site of a Saxon farm at Bradsole (a broad pond), and now in the 20th c. incorporated into a modern mechanised farm unit. After the Dissolution, some of the stonework was sold for building projects, in particular that of Sandgate Castle, built in 1539 but today much of the monastic stonework can still be recognised. The north wall of the tower is an entrance gate, the refectory is the farmhouse, the guest house is a barn, the well is covered but the 'broad' pond is once again a farm pond as it was in the Saxon monastic settlement.

On the other hand, nothing remains at Faversham except a record of its excavations, while at Boxley only the great tithe barn, a part of the outer wall and the scattered ruins of the church still stand. Even so, the

St. Radegund's Abbey, Bradsole.

finds have revealed its original plan. In churches, too, much religious symbolism was obliterated or destroyed, such as the painting of St. Thomas at Brookland and the frescoes re-discovered in the latter half of the nineteenth century above the chancel arch at Eastry. Maybe St. Augustine's, Canterbury epitomises for most of us the original wealth and glory of such religious houses and the destruction caused by their suppression. Apart from its great gateway, only the ruins of 'its broken arches, its mouldering pinnacles and the airy tracery of its half demolished windows' (Ingoldsby) remain for the modern pilgrim, the tourist, to see.

CHAPTER 38

'Bartholomew Fair at the Seaside'

MEREGATE (OR MARGATE) was once a small fishing village with a single long, irregular street, now called High Street. It grew at a passage to the shore through the line of chalk cliffs of the North Foreland. By 1700 it was a flourishing port trading in coal from the north-east and timber from the Baltic for Chatham Dockyard and half of the corn for London also left from Margate. The single carved wooden pier jutting out into the sea excluded the waves and wind from the north-east, but gave poor protection from south-westerly storms. Margate was also a good stepping-off point for the Continent; it was a port of embarkation to Holland for William of Orange and by the early nineteenth century, packet boats plied regularly across the Channel to Boulogne and Ostend.

Margate first became famous in the 1760's as a resort for London's holiday-makers. In 1766 Thomas Gray described it as 'Bartholomew Fair by the seaside'. By the early nineteenth century Margate had more visitors than any other seaside place in England. It was accessible from London by sailing vessels leaving Billingsgate on any tide for a twelve-hour journey to Margate Pier. With a head wind or becalmed, it could take two days. The journey has been described by many travellers. One visitor wrote: 'After tumbling and rumbling, tacking and re-tacking, we reached Margate. It was impossible to land at the pier through the lowness of the tide, so the boat put off...' Charles Lamb also wrote of 'the most agreeable holiday of my life' spent at Margate, after making the journey from London in the old Margate hoy with its 'weather-beaten, sun-burnt captain and his rough accommodation'. With the introduction of steam vessels in 1815, the journey took only 5 hours. Leaving London Bridge at 10.00 am, visitors could stroll along Margate's pier by mid-afternoon.

The invention of the bathing machine by Benjamin Beale, a local resident, was the culmination of Margate's fame as a London seaside resort. Bathing machines were first used there in 1790 and soon

114

bathing rooms had become big business, with seven built near the harbour to the west of the High Street. Imagine the scene: the bathers and their friends awaited their turn, perhaps reading the daily newspaper and discussing the gossip. Bathing had become a popular leisure pursuit and now doctors were advocating the health-giving properties of sea water. Horse-drawn carts plied between the bathing rooms and the machines, the drivers calling, 'Any more for the shore, please?' The cost was one shilling for two ladies or two shillings each with a guide. One record relates the experience. 'The "bathing machine" had a blue door and a very wet carpet inside. We felt insulted by having two towels handed to us which were no larger than sheets of blotting paper; the jogging box began to move and we were bumping about from side to side like a weaver's shuttle. At last we were in the sea with the waves splashing against the machine and making a gurgling noise among the wheels and shaking the door as if they were trying to come inside and wet our clothes.' It was not long before Margate had four marble salt-water baths filled with heated salt water at 3/6d. each or seven for a guinea.

In Margate at the height of the summer season we may easily forget the old Margate hoy, the wooden pier and Benjamin Beale's bathing machine. Yet there are street names such as Marine Parade, hotels like the Royal York and the Royal Albion, and the Golden Jubilee clock tower, the 1898 Hippodrome and the 'Hall by the Sea' not far from the stone pier and its bandstand and pavilion. All these and more are constant reminders of the earlier Margate's 'Bartholomew Fair at the seaside' fame.